THE DIALOGUE CONTINUES

THE DIALOGUE CONTINUES

Tales from the Making of Capilano College

editors

Bill Schermbrucker

Crawford Kilian

consulting editor

Pierre Coupey

CAPILANO UNIVERSITY FACULTY ASSOCIATION

THE DIALOGUE CONTINUES

CAPILANO UNIVERSITY FACULTY ASSOCIATION
Fir 501e, 2055 Purcell Way, North Vancouver, BC V7J 3H5
cfa@capilanou.ca

Library and Archives Canada Cataloguing in Publication

The dialogue continues : tales from the making of Capilano College / Bill Schermbrucker and Crawford Kilian, editors.

ISBN 978-0-9879052-4-6 (pbk.)

1. Capilano University—History. I. Kilian, Crawford, 1941–, editor II. Schermbrucker, Bill, 1938–, editor III. Capilano University Faculty Association, issuing body

LE3.C33D52 2014 378.711'33 C2014-902738-9

Cover image: Richard Whatley, *D is for Diploma* (1998), cast plaster with metal powders, wood, steel, 1m × 1m × 3m,
Installation photograph courtesy George Rammell, Studio Art Department

Cover and interior page design, layout, and typesetting:
Jan Westendorp, Kato Design & Photo

Printed in Canada by Island Blue Printorium Bookworks

To the colleagues, students, and
community who shared in the making
of Capilano College / University,
and to those who will
carry the task onward

CONTENTS

PREFACE

WHEN THOSE GOVERNING Capilano University began to shift the focus of the institution by vertical cuts of entire programs, I asked the Capilano Faculty Association how I could help. Film and Business are great departments! But what about Arts, Sciences, Studio Arts, Computer Studies and all the rest of the many diverse offerings that made Cap the respected comprehensive college / university that it was and should be?

John Wilson, long-time Chief Steward of the Faculty Association, bought me lunch and invited me to get people to tell their stories of how Cap was built.

That's what this book is, mostly written by retirees who still care passionately about Cap and want to see its traditions of excellence and comprehensiveness continued, not diminished.

My thanks to colleagues Crawford Kilian, Pierre Coupey, and Jan Westendorp, whose considerable involvement made this book possible.

BILL SCHERMBRUCKER

INTRODUCTION

No doubt it's a concern for professionals in any field as they approach retirement: They begin to realize how quickly institutional memory can fade. Younger colleagues take the status quo for granted, with little sense of how it was achieved and perhaps little sense of why that achievement mattered. For those stepping down, much remains unsaid, unexplained—perhaps the most important things.

Those of us who have retired from teaching at Capilano College / University were directly engaged in its creation and evolution, and we learned as much from the experience as we hope our students learned from us. It was hard-won knowledge, and it mattered because so much was at stake for all concerned: for us as individual teachers, because it affected our own lives and careers; for our students, because how we taught was at least as important as what we taught; for Capilano itself, because how we built it would determine its durability and resilience for decades to come.

Much of our knowledge, however, left the campus with us. And maybe that's a good thing in some ways: No one in 2014 could or should launch a new school on the principles and resources available to us in the 1960s, any more than we in 1968 should have built a school on the principles and resources available in 1926.

But it also means our younger colleagues must painfully rediscover what we learned in the 1960s and 70s, and the whole point of education is to spare young people the difficulty of reinventing the proverbial wheel.

As Capilano faces its latest crisis, some of us decided to develop one last lesson plan, based on our experience, in hopes of giving today's faculty, administrators, students, and public a little perspective on that crisis.

The thesis of the memoirs in this book is not that Cap is suddenly underfunded; we were underfunded from the start. The thesis is that faculty, not administration, have historically dealt with the problems of underfunding. Our responses have sometimes been inept and sometimes brilliant. They have invariably taken a long time to thrash out in endless meetings (sometimes held around an oil-drum heater on a cold picket line). They have made and broken friendships. Once finally reached, our solutions have sometimes lasted only a year or two. But sometimes they have lasted decades, and become institutionalized.

Early on, as young radicals, we improvised a kind of academic democracy that functioned regardless of academic hierarchy. Now, as old conservatives, we are trying to protect that democracy from those in the hierarchy who misunderstand not only Capilano but the changes in education and society since 1968. As a school approaching its 50th anniversary, Cap is too old to improvise and too young to die.

We did not build Capilano only to hand it over to those who think its teachers are merely "blathering on and lecturing people, [which] does not resonate with this generation" as its current president argued in the *North Shore News* late in 2013.

Cap faculty have experienced and promoted change in their classrooms from day one. We have known what resonates with students for almost half a century. Historically, Cap's teachers have driven change, often over administration foot-dragging.

We were the ones who saw the changes in our students and in society, and developed courses and programs to meet their needs. We went through several pedagogical and technological revolutions, and alerted our administrators about what was going on.

That's why faculty were developing their own departmental web pages, while administrators wondered about this whole internet thing. We were calling for more international students thirty years ago, but it took years before the administrators caught on.

As for "blathering on and lecturing at people," Cap's teachers from the very start were concerned about teaching skills that would reach everyone, from single mothers returning to work, to adult basic education students, to persons with disabilities. One reason we loved teaching at Cap was that we had to respond to new challenges constantly to meet our students' needs. Like standup comics, we had to read the room every day, watching for light bulbs or question marks to go on over student heads.

Historically, constructive change at Cap has come from the faculty up, not from the administration down. Our best administrators had Cap teaching experience; they knew what we could do. They saw their job as encouraging and channelling our innovations, and then finding the money for them. They did not see their job as cutting whole programs and departments, from the top down, on the pretext of change. The first instructional administrators, Les Brooks (Academic) and Harold Kirchner (Career / Vocational) encouraged open dialogue with faculty and support staff as well as College Council (board) members about what the institution should be doing and how. They held all-College retreats to places like the UBC Forestry camp at Haney, the

Alta Lake resort, Camp Elphinstone in Howe Sound and Paradise Valley outside of Squamish, where for several days, everyone sat around and talked and listened, developing a collective vision of the College's purpose and plans.

In this book, we have presented widely differing points of view on Cap's early years and development. Some of us have intensely personal memories to share; others have written mini-histories of their departments or programs, celebrating real educational achievements that would otherwise be forgotten.

Very roughly, we have alternated between the personal and the institutional, while sequencing the memoirs from the early days (when even typewriters were scarce) to modern dialogues expressed in email, which we could never have foreseen when Cap was founded.

No doubt we have missed much. But we believe our contributors have expressed a remarkably consistent vision of Capilano, whether as College or University, that deserves to live.

We thank the Capilano Faculty Association for supporting this book, and our colleagues for their contributions.

BILL SCHERMBRUCKER
CRAWFORD KILIAN
CO-EDITORS
SPRING 2014

THE VERY FIRST DAYS OF CAPILANO COLLEGE

TIM HOLLICK-KENYON

CAP COLLEGE WAS an "instant college." It was September, 1968.

There was no time then for planning, budgeting, policy formulation, or pensive thought.

At that time, it was required that a region desirous of a community college must first successfully win a referendum. The Chairman of that Committee to sell this concept was Peter Jones. He was a great man in many respects.

His message for the referendum campaign was "this college is for OUR CHILDREN." How could you knock Motherhood?

It passed.

The administrators hired at the outset were: Alf Glenesk, Principal; Leslie (Les) Brooks, Dean of Academic Studies; Harold Kirchner, Dean of Career Programs; Terry Donovan, Bursar; and myself as Dean of Student Services.

My first day on the job was a Friday in September, 1968. The next Monday would be the first day of Registration. We had absolutely no idea of how many bodies would walk through those doors. The rough planning estimate was for 300 students. The final student body count that semester was 678.

Those doors were a temporary complex attached to the West Vancouver Secondary School. The very first student to register, virtually "Number One," was Barbara Holloway. We maintained contact for many years. Sadly, Barbara passed away last year. She was a marvelous lady.

For the first year, Cap College classes started at 3:30 p.m. in the West Vancouver Secondary school building, after the high school students' day ended at 3:00 p.m. The level of cooperation with the secondary school administration was outstanding. Amazingly, it worked.

The first days of Cap College's existence were hectic and exciting. There was absolutely no policy to guide us. If a problem suddenly arose, there was a quick huddle, and the policy was formulated then and there! Instantly! My first registration forms for students were four-by-six-inch index cards that listed the courses that they had signed up for.

Class sections then were bundles of computer cards full of punched holes set up in cardboard boxes, usually consisting of twenty cards, with two cards held "in reserve". Les Brooks, Harold Kirchner and Bill Schermbrucker would hover nervously nearby, waiting for a section to fill up. Then they would dash upstairs and phone a prospective faculty member to inform them that they were hired!

On the second Monday, after Registration Week, Alf and I met to try and figure out exactly how to design a registration system. We did not have a clue. So I phoned Stan Evans, the SFU Registrar at that time. When I met Stan that day, he gave me all of their forms. I crossed out the university headings, wrote "Capilano College" over them, and sent them to their printer. We used the SFU Computer Centre for the first few semesters. Since we were the lowest on the SFU totem pole priority, my scheduled time to run our first marks was at 3:00 a.m. When I examined the first batch of student records, the GPA was missing! So the run was repeated. In those days, I personally checked every Statement of Grades before they were mailed out.

Slowly, the Student Services core group was hired. Rosemary Fell was the first secretary. Marilyn La Marre became the first counsellor, followed by Gary Siegrist and Bob Bagshaw. Later, Hersh Cramer and Dick Clarke came on board as Assistant Registrars. I processed the first student loan applications at home during the week-ends.

Interestingly, when we analyzed the very first registration statistics, forty per cent of the registrants were mature students. My basic criteria for admission to the College: if a person was nineteen years of age, and could see lightning and hear thunder, they were admissible as a mature student. This cohort made excellent students. Many a lady came to my office in tears, complaining that she had only got a B grade on her first essay!

The tuition fee for a resident student then was $20.00 per course. The funding formula then was based on a per-student enrolment, so the College quickly ballooned in size over the first few semesters. More classrooms were opened at Highlands United Church during the daytime. The first faculty hired were of extremely high academic quality. The first class sizes then were very small, so early students received a superior education.

Many of those first students went on to greatness. I meet them everywhere in our community. Last year, a former student contacted me. He ended up with a PhD from the London School of Economics via Harvard. Today he is in an Ottawa think tank, and consults informally with Prime Minister Harper. Early on, I developed a system with a social worker in the Ministry of Social Welfare whereby single mothers on welfare got their fees and textbooks covered by the provincial government. One former student earned a law degree and was hired by the Workers Compensation Board. Another student eventually earned a PhD in English, and taught at UBC. Two chiefs of the Squamish Band were early students.

The early college campus was in constant ferment. A student government was formed. A student newspaper arose. College retreats were held. The faculty were feisty. We created an Appeals Committee where a student could appeal a grade. The student filed a letter of appeal along with a fee of $5.00. The student and the faculty member appeared before a joint student-faculty committee of six persons. If the grade was changed, the $5.00 was returned to the student.

Those were heady days. Of course, there were disputes and problems along the way. But everybody cared! Obviously, the "instant college" became a great success. Today, we are witnessing the transition from a community college model to an evolving great university.

Views of the Capilano College portables at West Vancouver Secondary, 1968.

Early builders of Capilano College.
LEFT TO RIGHT: West Vancouver Mayor Alex Forst; Education Minister Donald Brothers; Principal Alf Glenesk; Dean of Instruction Leslie Brooks.

A typical Capilano College classroom at
West Vancouver Secondary School, circa 1968–69.

THE EMERGENCE OF THE CULTURE OF CAPILANO COLLEGE

CRAWFORD KILIAN

ALTHOUGH THE BC government had been under pressure for years to provide more access to post-secondary education, it was not until the spring of 1968 that a referendum endorsed a "North Shore College," which was soon named Capilano. By August 1968 the College was open, with a small cadre of administrators operating out of a couple of portables attached to the side of West Vancouver Secondary.

The key administrators, Principal Alf Glenesk and Dean Leslie Brooks, were dedicated to the idea of a community college, but knew they were creating Capilano almost from scratch. Les Brooks's experience was in adult education; Alf Glenesk had been vice-principal at the original Vancouver Community College at 12th and Oak, founded just three years earlier. I had met him there in my first year of college teaching, 1967–68.

That I was teaching at all was a reflection of the shortage of qualified post-secondary teachers in Vancouver (and across the country). I had immigrated to Canada from California early in August 1967 and was hired a few days later by VCC to replace another American, who had lasted two weeks before returning home. Apart from the desperation of the head of the English department, my chief qualification was that I was a Columbia University graduate and she had taken some summer courses there.

The culture of that early VCC was a mix of middle-aged former high school teachers whose master's degrees qualified them to teach post-secondary, with a few young MA's fresh out of grad school (or still in grad school). The College was based in the old King Edward High School building, where class photos going back decades still adorned the walls—partly because many of the senior faculty were in those class photos and had insisted they remain.

As a result, VCC was still struggling to get out of high school: it still had a principal, and in most classrooms students sat at desks on rails. But I can understand the feelings of the King Ed alumni: They had grown up in a distinctive and rewarding school culture and weren't ready to let it go.

VCC's mission included academic, university-transfer courses and career programs (Vancouver Vocational Institute was technically another campus of VCC but effectively autonomous). The administrators had spent their careers in public education, but this kind of post-secondary was new to them, and they were still feeling their way. So were faculty.

Moving to the brand-new Capilano College in August 1968, I found myself in a very different environment. VCC had soaked up many of the veteran high-school teachers, so Alf Glenesk and Les Brooks were obliged to hire whatever novices they could find. They got people very different from themselves.

While the first batch of faculty had a few people in their 40s, most of us were in our 20s and 30s, and in a year when our generation elsewhere was shaking the world: fighting on both sides of the Tet offensive in Vietnam, battling in the streets of Paris, and occupying the office of Columbia's president Grayson Kirk.

A number of us were from the US, still wrapped up in the politics of the old country (one was an army deserter); others were from Britain, Kenya, and far-flung parts of the Commonwealth.

The winners of World War II had all been busy disgracing themselves for years: the Soviets in Hungary and Czechoslovakia, the French in Indochina and Algeria, the British in Suez and Africa, and now the Americans in Latin America and Vietnam.

We may have been the victors' children, but we had little gratitude and less respect for what they'd made of their victory. (In *A Hard Day's Night*, Ringo cheeks a stuffy veteran: "Bet you're sorry you won.") Our arrogant self-righteousness may look silly now, especially since we had personally prospered in our countries' postwar success. But the alternative then seemed to be to cheer the napalming of Asian children.

Education as a public good, not just a private benefit

We had absorbed one principle from our parents' generation and their experience: Education was a public good more than a private benefit. Yes, graduates might earn more, and in prestigious occupations, but they also had an obligation to take a constructive part in democratic society. We had been educated as citizens, not as consumers, and we would try to convey that principle to our students. Yes, many of them were training for particular careers, but they would still be citizens. As Les Brooks observed during one of our early registration periods, "An education is an intellectual adventure." What students did for a living after that adventure, he went on, was up to them.

As well, we were increasingly aware of environmental issues. The Club of Rome issued its frightening report. Paul Ehrlich's book *The Population Bomb* alarmed many of us. In those days, autumn in Vancouver was marked by a stinging haze from loggers burning slash, and a beehive burner was still operating in

False Creek. Bob Hunter, the hip young *Vancouver Sun* columnist, was heralding a new environmental movement, and the Society Promoting Environmental Conservation was just getting started.

Our first intake of students, mostly white middle-class kids who hadn't made the cut for UBC or SFU, may have been unaware of such events and issues, but a few were already casualties of the world outside—like the Canadian veteran of Vietnam, with the first thousand-yard stare I'd ever seen, and the Iranian emigré who told me he was still scared of the Savak, the Shah's secret police. They were a portent of future waves of emigrés: Ismailis from Uganda, Vietnamese boat people, Czechs and Chileans. Capilano College would see them all.

We instructors, barely older than our students, felt we should prepare them for this dangerous world, though we had no clear idea how to do it. Many of us had marched in anti-Vietnam War demonstrations, to no discernible effect. The assassinations of Dr. Martin Luther King and of Bobby Kennedy seemed to mock any hope of social improvement. If anything, the violence and protests in the US in 1968—especially the Chicago police riot at the Democratic presidential convention—had further radicalized a generation without equipping it to create political change. Having been taught the theory of democracy, young Americans were unprepared for the practice of it in the 1960s.

(Meanwhile, a highly undemocratic convention of Liberal Party members chose Pierre-Elliot Trudeau as their next leader and therefore Prime Minister of Canada. As Northrop Frye once observed, "Canadians are Americans who reject the Revolution.")

It's a testimony to the maturity and patience of Alf Glenesk and Les Brooks that they didn't despair of us. While they might seem brusque or over-cautious, they taught us our jobs with a challenge here, an agreement there. In hindsight, they did a better job teaching us than we did with our students.

Understandably, the early years of Capilano College were a time of remarkable intellectual ferment. In addition to learning the elements of teaching, many of us were engaged in other fields as well. Some of us were writing; I recall timidly approaching Alf to see if it was OK for me to be writing radio plays for the CBC. (It was.) Bill Schermbrucker was writing novels as well as his PhD dissertation at UBC. Pierre Coupey, then a poet as well as a painter, launched *The Capilano Review,* and soon got himself in trouble with a cover featuring a faceless, full-frontal nude photograph.

Life in the bullpen

Ferment was inevitable, given our crowded conditions. In the two-storey portable grafted onto the front of West Van Secondary, a mob of mostly young instructors were thrown into a very small space: some two-person offices and a "bullpen" of desks available to whoever had no office.

We might work in different departments, but we lived communally. I shared an office with Penny LeCouteur of the Chemistry department, behind a bifold door without even a lock. Calls to faculty arrived at the front desk, where long-suffering secretaries shouted down the hall for us to come and pick up the phone. The English department begged for its own typewriter, so we could at least produce our own ditto masters for handouts. In a corner of the portable was a coffee room, and next to it a lounge with a tacky couch (still called a chesterfield in those days) upholstered in green vinyl, where meetings were held and naps taken. The chesterfield was to see long service even after the move to Lynnmour.

Quite apart from teaching our students, we were teaching one another. I gained an interest in Canadian literature in part from a young Simon Fraser professor, moonlighting at Cap, who would later oversee my master's degree in the subject.

Our students taught us as well: One of my earliest Cap students was a kid named Rod Marining, who was already past the hippie culture and moving into environmentalism. He became part of the crew on the ship that sailed north to protest nuclear tests at Amchitka (and that came back as the nucleus of Greenpeace). He would later take part in the protest that prevented a major development at the entrance to Stanley Park.

So while we didn't have anything quite like the faculty lunchroom at VCC, Cap did have the bullpen and the lounge as well as our classrooms as venues for teaching and learning. We exploited those resources daily.

We also faced unwelcome pressure from other institutions. UBC wanted to vet the English instructors who were teaching transfer courses. At least one career program was a kind of farm team for BCIT, right down to the BCIT-authorized textbooks. Gradually we developed our own programs and asserted some autonomy from UBC and SFU. And we tended to do this with the tacit approval of the administration, but not with its leadership. Instead, we went to curriculum meetings with the universities, argued our case, and won our own standing. It sometimes helped that many of us were grad students, with useful connections to university faculty.

This "do it yourself" attitude was in large part a reflection of our cramped quarters, which made it easy for faculty to share ideas and problems, as well as a natural development for a new institution with no traditions to get in the way. The attitude was to survive the move from West Vancouver to Lynnmour, where we finally found ourselves compartmentalized by division and program. The Social Sciences faculty chose to work in a single open area, now part of the library; after a year or two they dropped the idea as politically correct but unworkable. Humanities, where Continuing Education is now based, retained the old bullpen concept for part-time instructors, with rows of 2- and 3-person offices for full-timers.

From bull session to policy

To be compartmentalized by division was still to be thrown in with other faculty outside the English department, and we thrived on the exchange of ideas and experiences. Over thirty years later, as an emergency substitute instructor at Douglas College's David Lam campus in 2010, I was unpleasantly struck by the near-total lack of interaction between faculty, even those in adjoining offices. While the offices themselves were well-appointed, Douglas College's culture was quite different from the culture that emerged early at Capilano.

So when problems arose, everyone knew about them and had an opinion. Impromptu bull sessions sparked ideas that we then took back to our departments before they ever went to the deans.

The Communications department emerged in the mid-1970s through just such a process. English faculty tended to be given one or two or three sections of career-program English courses, regardless of their interest or experience in an already-specialized field. Many didn't enjoy such courses, and were frank in saying so to their colleagues. Meanwhile, faculty in career programs like Business and what was still called "Secretarial Science" were unhappy with their students' writing performance.

Casual bull sessions led to more serious discussions on whether to spin off the Communications courses from English and to run them out of an independent service program. The career programs liked the idea, and so did the English department. The College was expanding rapidly, so no one feared losing work, and a handful of instructors with both experience and interest in communications were quite willing to specialize. I wrote a proposal expressing the wishes of the relevant programs, and the administration rather promptly accepted it. It was a faculty-driven idea that solved some administrative problems.

This was a good example of the way the culture of Cap College dealt with a problem in the 1960s and 70s: The faculty would talk it over, frame a solution, and present it to an administration that was very willing to listen.

By contrast, top-down proposals from the administration, like the "directors" idea, were failures—not because faculty were bloody-minded, but because they didn't address recognized problems and hadn't been debated.

Greg Lee, a former faculty member, then an assistant dean, indiscreetly told me the directors would be "somebody we could fire" if things went wrong, and I quoted him in a hearing about the directors issue. The whole concept of "firability" reflected a growing gap between faculty and administration; the indiscretion itself reflected how close faculty and administration still were. And the administration's need to "fire somebody," rather than talk out the problem and find a solution, reflected how far apart from us they were growing. Greg survived his indiscretion to become a respected president of the College; as in many families, Cap's members forgive though they rarely forget.

The proxemics of Cap culture

The emerging administration-faculty culture was one of changing distances. In the first few years, the distance was generational—between older men, experienced in non-university education, and younger men and women who were anxious to hold on to their jobs. No doubt Alf Glenesk and Les Brooks were anxious to hold on to their jobs as well, and they put up with our early faculty follies with more patience than I would tolerate today. Looking back, I can see that a mutual attitude of affectionate exasperation characterized the relationship between administrators and faculty. To some extent that attitude seems to have survived, though the affection has worn a bit thin.

On the West Van campus the administrators were just down the hall, we could talk to them, and they would listen. Slightly later arrivals, like Harold Kirchner as Dean of Career Programs, were equally accessible. As a cynical young dope of 29, I thought Harold too enthusiastic; before long I came to understand the wisdom of his enthusiasm and the value of his support. He wanted us to succeed, not on his terms but on our own—which he often understood better than we ourselves did. I look back on him now as one of my own great mentors, and I hope my later teaching reflected his philosophy.

Capilano College moved to the Lynnmour campus in 1974, after years of administration campaigning for a site at the top of Capilano Road. Perhaps Alf and Les had wanted the maximum rainfall possible, but we were relegated to a slightly drier spot around a gravel pit overlooking Second Narrows Bridge. I recall suggesting Lower Lonsdale as a better spot: urban, embedded in the community like the great universities of Toronto and Montreal. My idea went nowhere. (The political masters of British Columbia knew what they were doing when they relegated UBC to Point Grey and SFU to the top of Burnaby Mountain: they didn't want students making trouble downtown, and Cap too was isolated like a suspected disease carrier.)

The first building, the Library, was soon enhanced by Arbutus, which became the centre for most of the administration. Meanwhile, a cluster of temporary buildings sprang up north of the Library, where most of the career programs were housed. We remained relatively close to our dean.

Space has always been a contentious issue at Cap: We always had too little, and what little we had faced conflicting demands. Like Los Angeles freeways, each ugly new concrete addition seemed only to encourage more traffic jams. Their names were banal—Maple, Fir, Cedar, and Birch; after a decade or two, we had enough history to justify a Glenesk Building or a Brooks Hall. At least we have a music room named for Harold Kirchner, but Capilano has never been comfortable with the deaths of its people. We have preferred to mumble an acknowledgement, maybe set up a scholarship fund, and then forget them.

Well, those were administrative decisions, as was the decision to move all the administrators from Arbutus to the fourth floor of Birch—an ugly slab of concrete and glass, with a spectacular view of the South Campus parking lot and the oil refinery across Burrard Inlet. At this point the proxemics—the use of space to communicate—sent a clear message: the administration would be a world unto itself, looking away from the campus or merely across to its own north wing. Faculty and students were relegated to increasingly overcrowded classrooms and cramped offices.

An increasing number of administrators were being drawn from faculty ranks, a trend that would persist. While we joked about such colleagues' departures for "the dark side," we appreciated that they had shared a great deal of experience with us. But just as moving from the role of student to that of teacher can cause a dramatic change in attitude, the move to administration changed our colleagues' attitude as well.

This is not to say that faculty and administration were estranged. But each group now had its own space and its own culture, each insulated from the other. Faculty could meet with administrators in the conference room on the fourth floor of Birch, and deans could visit department meetings in Cedar or Fir, and they could accomplish a great deal. Even so, these would be statements of positions, rather than conversations leading to a consensus.

Sheer proxemics kept administrators on one team and faculty on another. If some early decision had put the deans down the hall from the departments they ran, they would have evolved as spokespersons for their departments to their fellow-administrators. They would have been more forceful advocates for their departments, and more forceful advocates for the administration as well. Just as coordinators often have to speak bluntly to their faculty, an administrator seen as "on side" by faculty carries more persuasive force.

A college in a community

We were, through the 1970s and 80s, very much a community college. The vast majority of our students lived in North and West Vancouver. "Foreign students" were recent immigrants or an occasional stray from Hong Kong. The Squamish and Sechelt campuses served their own communities. We continued to provide a wide range of arts and science programs as well as career training. Capilano prospered in the 1970s in the rapid expansion of the community-college system under the NDP's Dave Barrett, and suffered in the early 1980s recession and the Socreds' restraint policy.

By now the faculty were a full-fledged union, and we even went on strike once or twice. However acrimonious faculty and administration relations might be, we always came to a resolution of our disputes and carried on.

In the academic pecking order, community colleges were very much a step down from the universities. We had experienced university snobbishness in our early years, and it remained an issue. I recall one time when I volunteered to go out to talk to UBC grad students in the English department about college teaching as a career option for them. They gave me a polite hearing, asked a few questions, and left. Only one of them followed up, and he eventually became a Communications instructor. But even as the universities began to overproduce people with advanced degrees, those graduates were holding out for jobs in universities that would permit them to overproduce still more graduates.

Our own culture had tendencies in the same direction: university transfer programs seemed to have more cachet than career programs. This could be an annoyance, but it was little more than sibling rivalry. Besides, many faculty migrated from one to the other, or happily carried a workload divided between them.

Still, as years passed the sibling rivalry became more like competing bureaucracies, fighting for money. Having cast my lot with the career programs, I supported them while wishing the UT programs every success. Being more "practical" and "job-oriented," Careers could usually count on provincial support for new programs and even stand-alone courses. My own Communications department was essentially a cluster of service courses, each designed to meet the needs of some particular program. But even we could run a few "open" sections of courses like magazine article writing, and keep those sections even if enrollment was light (it was usually strong).

That required administration support, and I usually got it. Harold Kirchner was running Careers; our morale was high largely because he kept his coordinators very much in the loop and protected sections with light enrollments. Division meetings were monthly, held in his home after a good lunch. Everyone got to know everyone else, we brainstormed ideas to solve problems, and life went well.

Underfunding plus inflation

This was no utopia on the hill, however. We had started out underfunded, and so we remained. The NDP in the early 1970s had used soaring resource revenues to expand the college system, but we never seemed to have enough to meet the demands on us. The Socreds after their return to power in 1975 were reluctant as ever to maintain funding.

By the early 1980s we were contending not just with tight budgets, but with endless inflation. I was then a North Vancouver school trustee, and we felt very pleased to sign a contract with our teachers in 1981 at precisely the provincial average for settlements: a raise of 15 per cent.

Then the US jacked up interest rates to induce a recession,

cooling off inflation—but at a high cost to the North American economy, including British Columbia's. The recession's impact on BC was brutal, and led to the notorious restraint program in 1983. Despite the protests of civil servants, police and firefighters, and despite the BCTF going on strike, the Socreds' cutbacks remained.

Paul Gallagher, then our president, was told by some government apologist to "do more with less"—not the first time, and certainly not the last, that BC educators have been so advised. Gallagher, usually a diplomatic man, pointed out that Capilano College had been doing more with less all its life.

By early 1983 I was no longer on the school board; campaigning for re-election, I had met voter anxiety face to face. People thought cutting spending would at least reduce their tax burden a little, and that was enough inducement to support right-wing candidates. As it turned out, being kicked out of elective office was a blessing: I went to the Vancouver *Province* and pitched myself as an education columnist. They had no one on the beat, and freelancers were cheaper than staffers, so I spent over ten years as a columnist—a job that got me invited all over BC to meet educators and learn more about a system far more complex than I had ever imagined.

Of course I criticized the restraint program and its Socred authors, but Capilano's administration fully supported me. Paul Gallagher got at least one letter from an angry Socred, demanding that I be silenced. He quietly let me know about the letter, adding that he would not be responding to it.

In the summer of 1983 I took a leave of absence and went to China with my wife and children, replacing another Capilano faculty member at the Guangzhou Institute of Foreign Languages.

It was supposed to be a year's appointment, but we lasted one semester and came home to rescue our children's school year. This was to be one of the first of Capilano's ventures to China. While it was unsuccessful (I was woefully unprepared for teaching in China, and the Chinese themselves weren't quite clear on how to use foreign teachers), it was also highly instructive. I came home keenly aware of the potential for trade and cultural exchange between Canada and China.

For months thereafter I was a bit of a China bore, urging my colleagues and the administration to find ways to attract Chinese students to Cap, and thereby to start forming the ties of *guanxi*, the network of relationships that China runs on. My dreams would eventually come true, though not in the way I'd hoped.

While my family and I were in China, BC teachers had gone on strike and scores of thousands of protesters had surrounded the Socred convention in the Hotel Vancouver. The Solidarity movement seemed to be re-radicalizing teachers. But it was not to last.

In one of my *Province* columns after my return, I reported on how I had heard about Premier Bill Bennett's resignation: while listening to David Suzuki speaking to a large crowd in the new BC Place Stadium. I had been writing my first book on our education problems, *School Wars*, which I naively thought might sway a few voters by listing the Bennett government's deliberate harm to the system.

But as I left BC Place, itself a monument to Socred triumphalism, I reflected that Bennett's government had determined how we would move around the building and how we would function thereafter in the BC the Socreds had made. Bennett had dug the channels, and we must follow them whether we liked it or not.

So I was not that surprised when Bill Vander Zalm became

premier (and he did fund post-secondary surprisingly well); the topography of BC education had been set, and money would flow where the Socreds had decreed. The arrival of Mike Harcourt and Glen Clark in the 1990s made little difference.

Moving into a new world

We were now moving into a new world. In 1989 the Soviet bloc imploded, followed by the USSR itself in 1991. We had also seen Chinese students crowding into Tiananmen Square, and then slaughtered. Communism by the end was a pretty shabby threat, but for 70 years it had offered an alternative that capitalism had been forced to deal with, whether with blacklists or with decent salaries.

Freed of this burden, capitalism began to rethink its relationship to the public sector. If paying for education was no longer an absolute cost of doing business, then continuing to pay for it would depend on getting a decent return on the investment.

So in our meetings with administration at Capilano, we began to get the message: Every class had to be full. Students would pay a bigger share of the costs of their investment, regardless of the benefit of an educated public. A section, a course, or a program that couldn't enroll enough warm bodies was to be sacrificed. Programs that could offer good chances of employment were supported.

We were now a kind of education mall, with each program a tenant flogging a particular line of goods. A tenant that couldn't pay the rent would soon be gone.

Whether Socred, NDP, or Liberal, successive BC governments drove that home. Never mind that even our brightest career-program students didn't always end up in the jobs they'd been trained for. It *looked* as if our programs were now designed to support BC employers, freeing them from the expensive tedium of training their own employees. And, politically speaking, looks were what mattered.

A very expensive lottery ticket

However radical we faculty may have fancied ourselves, we had always worked hard to serve the universities, employers, and the public in general. We did so now, even through the dark ages of the Gordon Campbell government. To our amazement, that government jacked up tuition costs and still the students poured in. The Liberals understood the situation better than we did: Post-secondary education had been a passport to a safe career for us, but now it was nothing more than a lottery ticket for such a career. Kids had to mortgage their lives in the hope that a degree might make a difference of a million dollars or so in their lifetime incomes. Young people who wouldn't or couldn't pay the fee would give up even the hope of living as well as their parents had.

I well recall Greg Lee explaining the current funding situation in a Faculty Association meeting sometime in the mid-2000s. "In other words," I responded, "the beatings will continue until morale improves." Greg laughed along with the faculty, but the beatings continued and morale did not improve.

Right from the summer of 1968, a key element of Capilano College's culture had been job anxiety: the fear of losing a really good job, a job with the chance for a real career. For anyone who really loved teaching, Cap was as good as it got. But job anxiety didn't end with a union and regularization. Coupled with it was anxiety for one's program: How could we attract more students, hire more teachers, and make ourselves financially safe against political misfortunes?

This aspect of our culture flourished at the turn of the century. Business Administration reveled in funding for Microsoft training until the dot-com bubble burst, and faculty lost their jobs or returned to teach more tedious subjects. Tourism Management began to ship students to Vietnam; as the paper chase intensified, it developed a degree program, ensuring that two-year grads would return for a better piece of paper.

From citizens to consumers

If we had shown enterprise in our early years in devising ways to turn students into citizens, we showed far more enterprise in schemes to turn students into consumers—especially of our services.

Again, the onus was on faculty to come up with the ideas and to pitch them to administration. My own Communications department did just that, winning support first for a certificate program in the subject and then for a degree. As we had been a farm team for BCIT in 1968, we became the farm team for Simon Fraser's Communications program 40 years later. And we were grateful.

Meanwhile the College was finally making the Asian connections I'd dreamed of in the 1980s. Suddenly the cafeteria was full of kids chattering away in Farsi, Korean, Japanese, and Chinese. Once a suburban school, we had become a cosmopolitan hub for foreign students willing to pay in full for the high cost of their education.

This was both a blessing and a curse: Foreign students enlivened our classes and challenged us to find new teaching methods. But those same students were soon paying so much that they were subsidizing sections and courses for Canadian students. Capilano was as eager as any other post-secondary to attract foreign students, but before long we actually depended on them for much of our revenues. Our original mandate as a college for our community was being ignored. We were being semi-privatized, driven to sustain ourselves by outside funding. It was not, and is not, a healthy situation.

I was glad to see my department flourishing while other programs were fighting for their lives. But I played little part in our transformation; a colleague, Leslie Savage, was coordinating the department, and working hard to make these new programs happen. I was planning my retirement. For forty years I had had a wonderful time and been paid for it. Teaching at Cap had taught me more than I could have imagined when I went in for my first interview with Les Brooks.

However grim the grading might be on the weekends, however often I had to explain "i before e except after c" over four long decades, Capilano College kept challenging me with something new: a new course to build from scratch, or a program like nothing anyone had done before. That was how we began, and readiness for challenges remains part of the Capilano culture.

It had been no ivory tower; I often think of Yuri, the Outdoor Rec student who was trying and failing to rebuild his life after his Canadian Forces unit was accidentally bombed one night outside Kabul in 2002. He was the spiritual son of the Canadian Vietnam vet I'd taught in 1969, the quiet young man with the thousand-yard stare.

Of course we had failed, in our cozy suburban redoubt, to prevent future Vietnams. However much we loved our students, and however much they loved us, they went on to vote for a succession of governments that despised us and all we stood for.

When the flat-screen monitors in the Sportsplex flashed "CAPILANO UNIVERSITY," and the confetti cannons went off, and everyone cheered, it felt as if the college we'd built for forty years was gone in forty seconds of cheers and applause. How far gone we would not learn for another six years: In April 2014, it was finally revealed in the *North Shore News* that the provincial government, in the spring of 2008, had reneged on its promises of $6.3 million in transition funding and $6 million in annual base funding. According to a Cap-commissioned report written in 2012, the administration had to sign off a new deal without any new money.

"The senior leadership of Capilano," wrote report author Don Avison, ". . . quite literally on the eve of the finalization of decision and the subsequent commencement of announcements felt they had no choice but to comply."

In hindsight, we can now see that the administration certainly had a choice: to refuse an impossible deal. Instead, administration not only signed off on a bad agreement; they continued to let Cap run on fumes for six years, pretending to be a full-fledged university while they cut courses and eliminated programs. Surely they must have known the truth would come out eventually. Perhaps they consoled themselves with the thought that they would be safely gone by then; their successors would take the blame and deal with the distrust.

But cultures are stubborn things; they outlast kingdoms and empires because they give life a meaning and direction it would otherwise lack. They even outlast their failures. The present situation is just the latest challenge Cap has offered its faculty, staff, and students, not to mention its administration. The do-it-yourself culture of the early Capilano College had its problems, but it *worked*. It built not only values, not only programs and courses, but institutions. Those institutions have survived many hard times, and will survive many more—if the Capilano community recalls its roots, understands how deep they run, and builds on them.

Capilano College Council, 1968
LEFT TO RIGHT: Dr. John Ellis, William Lucas, A.H. Glenesk (Principal), Peter Jones (the West Van Mayor and Chairman), Bae Wallace, J.M. McDonald, Bill Manson.
BILL McPHEE PHOTO

An early faculty-administration meeting, probably in the West Van Secondary library. Identifiable persons, FROM LEFT TO RIGHT: Alf Glenesk (in glasses), Art Pape, Leslie Brooks, Keith Wade, Brad Van Huizen, Margaret Andrews.

TOP: Sod turning at Lynnmour campus, November 23, 1972. LEFT TO RIGHT: W.J. Wallace, Chairman, College Council; North Vancouver District Mayor Ron Andrews; Mary Griffiths, President, College Student Society; Sonja Sanguinetti, President, Capilano College Faculty Association; Principal Alf Glenesk.

LEFT: Harold Kirchner, Dean of Career Programs, March 1973.

THE STUDIO ART PROGRAM FROM BEGINNING TO END

BARRY COGSWELL

It is now quite certain that by the summer of 2014 the Capilano University Studio Art Program will be no more. It is a shameful and pathetic end to a program that has, over the years, touched greatness. Along with that program, Capilano's Textile Arts Program will also be cut. That program is unique in British Columbia and will be, in some ways, an even greater loss than Studio Art.

Both programs had their genesis as a range of courses in the first Capilano College Art Program, which ran from 1970 until approximately 1980. That program, which began in a large and modern warehouse on Welch Street, was a brave attempt to combine all the visual arts into one department. At first sight, that appears to be a very logical combination. However, it didn't work, and a move to separate into more philosophically compatible groupings became an imperative. Furthermore, the second permanent building constructed on the Lynnmour campus, the Arbutus building, and designed specifically to house only the Administration and the Art program, was opened in 1976.

Designing the first building to accommodate the Art Program indicates how strongly the administration then supported the College's art offerings. But the new building had a number of disadvantages. The first was that it was shared with the College administration. The clean suits and secretaries were somewhat slow to embrace the concept of clay-covered students stomping up and down the newly carpeted corridors, and paint and charcoal trodden into the carpets did little to help. Also the administrators felt some disappointment when they found the hand washing basins in the washrooms decorated with paint from the students' brush-cleaning endeavours. However, the sounds of grinding steel and hammering rock were wonderful at preventing the secretaries from focusing too much on those other annoying trivialities.

In designing Arbutus, attempts had been made to satisfy the specific requirements of the sculpture and pottery disciplines, but in most essentials the teaching of studio courses had to be undertaken in what were, in reality, standard classrooms next to administrators' offices. It was very soon realized, at least by the Studio Art instructors, that art and administration had somewhat incompatible requirements.

In this disillusioning atmosphere, and after a slow, protracted divorce, the division of one program into three was completed in 1981. The three new programs at that time were Studio Art, Crafts, and Commercial Art. However, in the College Calendar all were still listed under the Art Program with all faculty listed together under that heading. It took another twelve years, until 1993, before the faculties of the three programs were listed separately.

Immediately following the initial split, the Commercial program was the most secure. It had the promise of jobs with paid employment as an enticement to potential students. At the time Studio Art and Crafts were the poor relatives, with registration numbers being just over the minimum required. It was clear that Studio Art had to upgrade its profile and reputation if the program was to prosper. The subjects taught were drawing, painting, sculpture, printmaking, design, and art history.

Initially, the program faculty was composed of Wayne Eastcott, Ted Kingan as coordinator, David Marshall, Alan Wood, and me. Frank Molnar occasionally taught painting, but had most of his workload in the graphics program. After some time Alan Wood moved to Emily Carr and was replaced first by Gary Pearson, then by Allison Clay, and finally, in 1989 by Nancy Boyd. Not to be forgotten, and of great importance to the success of the students, were Bob Wiley, our printmaking tech Bonnie Jordan, and Dwane Neuberger, the tech in the sculpture department. Ann Rosenberg and Josephine Jungic from Humanities taught Art History.

The teaching strategies we employed were more technically based and more rigorously applied than in most other art programs at the time. This approach was vindicated by the high quality of student work that resulted. The faculty was quick to take advantage of these results by having annual off-campus exhibitions, for several years at Robson Square, to showcase the quality of works being produced.

The good press we received was stunning. The program's overall strategy also assumed that each student would eventually find his / her own individual form of expression quite independent of the specific subjects taught. It was taken for granted that after completing the program the grads would, based on new knowledge gained, go on to study in fields most suited to each individual, be that sculpture or architectural embellishment, painting, jewelry or furniture design. Most continued their graduate studies at university art programs across Canada.

Two outstanding students who come to mind from the early phase, when the program was located in Arbutus, are Michael Carmichael, who tragically passed away early, and Davide Pan.

Davide, for his 3rd year, went to the Accademia di Belle Arti in Venice where, in his first term, he won the Bevilaqua La Masa award. His submitted work was purchased by the City of Venice for the permanent collection of the Ca Pesaro, Venice Museum of Modern Art. He returned to Vancouver to a successful career as a sculptor. Some of his recent works were selected for the Artisti Italiani nel Mondo in the Venice Biennale 2011.

A new home

Over the years in the Arbutus building, it had become apparent that the program needed to move into better facilities and thereby grow. I had been coordinating the program since the early eighties by then, and it was clear to me that a certain empty building on campus would be perfect for our needs. That building had first been built to accommodate welding and house-construction programs, which had been closed after a year or two. I pestered the administration to make the building available to Studio Art, and after many rejections, I wrote one final letter to President Doug Jardine. That did the trick.

We were given the two huge empty spaces, with 22-foot high ceilings, into which we could move. Working closely with the architects, the faculty designed exactly how we wanted the large spaces partitioned. We were able to define the amenities that each discipline required, and also to design an integrated art gallery that proved to be an important teaching adjunct. In the summer of 1989 Studio Art moved into what was then arguably the most suitable, as well as the most beautiful, post-secondary art studio space in the lower mainland. At that point David Marshall retired and George Rammell was hired.

In 1990 Studio Art introduced the Art Institute. This was a program for post-graduate and practicing artists that gave them access to the printmaking and sculpture studios and equipment. The studios were available to the Art Institute participants at any time when they were not in use by 1st and 2nd level classes. The Art Institute was a great strengthener to the SART program, with Institute members acting as mentors to the students.

Throughout this time the faculty members considered it vital to individually engage in local and international exhibitions and symposia. For instance, Nancy Boyd had annual exhibitions of new work at the John Ramsay Gallery and later at Ballard / Lederer as well as at four public galleries in the Lower Mainland. Marcus Bowcott, who joined the faculty in the early 90s, exhibited at the Bau-Xi in both Vancouver and Toronto as well as in other commercial, public and alternative galleries. Since 1979 Wayne Eastcott exhibited in Japan and other international galleries, the most recent being at the Prince Takamado Gallery, Embassy of Canada, Tokyo. George Rammell exhibited in Vancouver, was invited to sculpture symposia in Helsingborg, Sweden and Brittany, France, and was Artist in Residence in the Austrian Alps. Earlier I had had two one-person shows at the Vancouver Art Gallery and represented Canada at the Raume und Installationen, Kunstler aus Kanada, Stuttgart, West Germany in 1983.

Word spread about the quality of Cap's Studio Art Program, and soon students were applying from beyond the lower mainland and from outside British Columbia. At that time, beginning in the mid 1980s and by the early 1990s, the student applicants had grown to approximately four times the numbers that we could accept. By rigorously selecting the most suitable students the learning outcomes and quality of graduating work reached new levels of excellence, levels which we diligently maintained.

Once in the new SART building, the program began to hold annual grad shows there. We took advantage of those opportunities to have the first-year students strip all the large studios of furniture, clean and paint the walls, and assist the second-year graduating students to hang their work. This gave the students great learning opportunities as well as giving the program the advantage of moving into a freshly painted clean building at the beginning of each new academic year.

The turnout at grad was always huge, with many hundreds attending. Such artists as Gordon Smith, Greg Snider from SFU and Liz Magor from ECUAD, among others, were guest speakers at Grad. Every year the reviews were most favourable. Visitors often commented on the advanced quality of the work coming out of this two-year program, remarking that the work often paralleled that of longer degree-granting programs.

With only one first- and one second-year group of students, the Studio Art Program was actually quite small when compared with Emily Carr and some other art programs. A sign of the quality of the program was that we had very few dropouts over the years. In fact the students went away from Cap with a sincere loyalty and attachment to the depth of their educational experiences and to their peers and the faculty who nurtured them. We often enjoyed return visits from alumni who would regale us with stories of how their fellow students at other institutions were in awe of our grads' skills, expertise and knowledge.

In many ways the SART building was a unique environment on campus. Where else did students, with the instructor on hand, work through the night to complete their first-semester sculpture projects? And where else on campus could they camp out overnight in the gallery for weeks before grad? How many drawing students had large dogs as life models? And, how many other instructors would have had the interest, and the energy, to bring to the building a live hay-munching horse for the second-year students to draw? On that occasion the horse was quite content until the instructor, when talking about the anatomy of the head, brought out the skull of another horse. The live horse clearly knew what he was looking at and didn't like it one bit. He tried desperately to bolt out of there. Aside from such notable occasions, for the students the time was mostly spent in intensely hard study, sublime creativity, comradeship, and fun.

The SART faculty members at that time were Marcus Bowcott, Nancy Boyd, Wayne Eastcott, George Rammell and me. Josephine Jungic and Dorinda Neave joined as the art history instructors. The techs were Merrell Gerber, Bonnie Jordan, Dwane Neuberger and Jack Ploesser.

International successes

During that maturing phase of the program, and in later years too, we had some notable student successes. Sawan Yanghwe and Dougal Graham showed their collaborative paintings in Europe for several years. Elizabeth Zvonar is now a new-media art star. Michele Smith went on to curate at the Tate in London. Dianne Espiritu runs her own design firm. Larissa Fassler is a very successful artist working in Berlin. The list goes on, but it is enough to say that many of our students had great success in the art world. However, I choose to believe that the ultimate manifestation of the value and success of Studio Art is illustrated by the large number of students who went out into the larger realm and were able to engage the opportunities and problems of our modern world with imagination, creativity and courage.

In 1993, ceramics became part of SART with Donalda McLaren as the instructor and Jack Ploesser as the ceramics tech. A few years later ceramics moved from the Arbutus building to the recently vacated old cafeteria close to the SART building. Sam Kwan oversaw the development of the classes, including the introduction of a Ceramics Institute. In 1998 Tiki Mulvihill joined the faculty when I had a one-year sabbatical. In 2003 Toni Latour was brought into the program to develop Media Arts courses. Then, as some of us retired, new people joined the faculty.

All of these additional faculty members had active art practices and were highly regarded professionals in their respective disciplines. When news of the closing of the Studio Art Program was announced, the SART faculty members were Marcus Bowcott, Ying-Yueh Chuang, Toni Latour, Tiki Mulvihill, Maria Anna Parolin, George Rammell, and Nicola Tibbetts. The technical assistants were Mike Babiarz, Katie Day, Merrell Gerber, Ben Lee, and Dirk Heiss.

For the final ten years the SART faculty chose to elect a coordinator from outside the program. First Sandra Seekins from Art History and then later Sandra Ferens from the Theatre program were chosen to coordinate.

Through the years, the campus community enjoyed provocative and impressive sculptures around campus, produced either by students, Institute members or faculty members, past and present. Most of the student pieces will have been retrieved by now but many pieces remain, including my steel sculpture on the public space outside the library. Outside in the woods by the

Fir Building is a piece by David Marshall, whose work is enjoying a resurgence several years after his death. Inside campus buildings, there are many beautiful works of art donated to the Capilano Art Advisory Committee Collection, works generously offered largely by faculty, their peers in the community or friends of the program. Pierre Coupey, for instance, though he taught in the English department, was once a Printmaking Institute member and always an unfailing friend to SART. He donated important paintings from his internationally acclaimed body of work. All the collection pieces that remain throughout the campus are beautiful, poignant reminders of the strength of the Studio Art Program when it flourished and, sadly, in the future will be reminders of its regretted absence.

Discussions about developing SART into a four-year program had taken place many times since the early 1990s. During 2012, a proposal for a degree program was being firmed up for presentation to the administration. After receiving a draft of this proposal in 2013, the administration offered no response to the department. Now we know why. They had other plans in the works, and those did not include either Studio Art or Textile Arts.

The present instructors, and all those who preceded them, along with many hundreds of fine students who truly understand the worth of Studio Art, will be mourning the loss of a unique and cherished program. It is a terrible shame that a shortsighted decision can destroy a program of such excellence. It is a further shame that the enthusiasm, dedication and diligence of all those who built and maintained the program, the past and present faculty, technicians and students, are apparently held in so little regard by the new university administration.

MY CAP MEMOIR

REID GILBERT

WHAT CONSISTENTLY pleased me as I began to become more deeply involved in the Canadian and international academy in the 1980s, 90s, and into the early twenty-first century was the high regard in which Capilano was held by what are now called "research universities." As I joined various academic associations and began to attend national and international conferences, I was always struck by the fact that people knew our college's name and considered it an intellectually important school.

For example, at a meeting of the Canadian Association for Theatre Research (then known by another name) at the Congress of the Social Sciences and Humanities (then called by the charmingly archaic name, "The Learned Societies Meetings") in 1993, a panel on employment opportunities for graduate students was convened. The notion of working in "a college" was floated and, predictably, the newly emerging PhDs were horrified at the prospect, exclaiming that they would not be able to do research, or write, or be among gifted professors.

I was personally chuffed (naturally), but also very proud of my school when one of the most prestigious of theatre scholars in Canada replied, "Nonsense. Look at Reid Gilbert—he's in that excellent college in Vancouver and his publishing record is very strong." I was asked to comment, and I noted the degree of practical support I received from Capilano: it was more modest than some scholars from major universities, but more generous than that offered by many of the smaller universities and colleges.

More important, I noted the high degree of intellectual and personal support from colleagues, my department and—then—the College administration.

In his tenure as President, Douglas Jardine was determined to see Capilano emerge as a strong, up-to-date academic institution. I was given release time, at one point, to design a long-term professional development plan and it was thoroughly discussed through the institution. I was encouraged in my idea of creating a series of extra-classroom lectures and seminars for interested students we called *ChatLive*, and my colleagues volunteered time to plan and animate these noon-hour sessions.

Throughout my career, I was encouraged to develop innovative teaching methodologies including early uses of word processing for composition: this initiative was marked by the American academy in conferring a Master Teacher's Award on me in 1991 and an Excellence Award in 1992, both at convocations at the University of Texas at Austin. At both ceremonies, Capilano was acknowledged as a singular institution, known for its scholarship and its commitment to teaching.

As I began to publish on Canadian theatre and performance theory, I was asked to speak at a number of international conferences; Capilano was always known when I arrived at institutions such as The University of Dublin, The University of Moscow, Rhode Island University, Harvard, The University of California, Berkeley, the University of Long Island, the University of the Netherlands, L'Université Libre de Bruxelles, Canterbury University, and many Canadian universities.

I first spoke at a national conference in 1977 and read papers at 24 institutions, most recently as Faculty Emeritus of Capilano University in 2011: I was always nourished by Capilano and its then administration throughout all those years. Since retiring, I have been appointed Adjunct Professor of Theatre at the University of British Columbia and, when I was first asked to teach a course there, the Head said, "You taught all those years at Capilano—we know you can do the job." This was the reputation of our school from its developing years forward.

Many of my colleagues were highly successful in other, similar academic, Creative Writing and Fine Arts worlds, and in areas of Science and the Social Sciences. Programs like InfoTech were leaders in the early exploration of new media. Music Therapy garnered national praise. Numbers of other special subjects were established to wide acclaim; Capilano was well known and highly regarded. It was a joy and a source of pride to be associated with Capilano.

Of course we had heavy teaching loads—heavier than those of the people with whom I was reading papers on panels—and almost never any research assistance (I did once have a research assistant for a major project for *The Capilano Review* and was able to hire research assistance during work on the second edition of my text, *A Short Guide to Writing about Literature*, though she was paid by my publisher). It was not easy to find time and energy to publish—but the evident support of my colleagues eased that burden. I felt encouraged to write; I breathed in a highly intelligent atmosphere that urged creativity; I was surrounded by achievers.

Over the years, I have published more than 90 articles and reviews, a play and two editions of a text at Pearson-Longman. I continue to serve on the Editorial Boards of two journals and also continue, in retirement, as an Associate Editor of *Canadian Theatre Review*.

Working at a college rather than a major university did not deter my desire to research and write, nor hamper my doing so; at least, working at the Capilano of my day did not. In 2011, I was awarded the International Chair Professorship at L'Université Libre de Bruxelles (Brussels University). The University of British Columbia marked that honour, announcing my appointment on its website and at a reception. Capilano University did not acknowledge this award, nor publicize the achievement of one of its *emeriti*. Times change, but a supportive, intellectually rigorous, and rewarding environment should not be lost. The younger faculty at Capilano University deserve the support I enjoyed. Capilano University deserves to be great.

AICHI GAKUSEN: A TRANS-PACIFIC EXCHANGE

NICK COLLINS

IN THE VERY EARLY 1980s, the then Principal of Capilano College, Paul Gallagher, received out of the blue a letter from Japan which would be a real game- or even life-changer for those associated with his response. The letter came from Aichi Gakusen (AG), a prestigious college in central Japan, one of the first to accept women into post-secondary study. It was looking for a sister institution in North America. The initial proposal was to set up a student exchange program. Gallagher's response was, "Why not?"

Within months a faculty committee was formed with instructors from Biology, History, German, Business and ESL. The committee reported directly to the president and had full autonomy in its operations.

For the time spent on the Japanese Exchange Committee (JEC), faculty were directly rewarded with a dinner during the evening of the interviews, and a formal dinner each September to welcome the Aichi students and hand out the plane tickets to the departing Capilano students. In addition, the returned Capilano students were invited and expected to order the meal in Japanese. All in all, it was a great annual event of celebration.

President Doug Jardine for 10 years, and President Greg Lee for 15 years, were both outstanding in their strong support of the committee and its work, as was Madeleine Adeoba as the staff member who supported the program with admirable commitment. It was a faculty committee that worked independently and reported directly to the president.

The program and its successful growth also saw the creation of a faculty exchange that for the past 20 years has sent a Capilano faculty member to visit Aichi Gakusen in May. Capilano provides financial support towards the airfare and AG provides room and board in a host family, as well as extensive support and superb hospitality. Faculty from all areas of Capilano have benefitted—Environmental Science, Art History, Global Stewardship, English, Geography and ESL have all sent faculty.

For faculty, being hosted by AG means that many doors, normally not open (or not opened quickly) to foreigners, are opened. Visits and contacts are arranged and this exchange has continued to bear fruit for the participants for many years afterwards.

The variety of Capilano students who travelled to Japan is impressive—applications were accepted from any student registered in any program at Cap. The key criterion was a genuine interest in Japan and what a student could take to Japan from Canada and bring back to Canada from their experience. Winners were judged holistically on their personal qualities, experience and values. In addition to a willingness to study Japanese before departing, students read prescribed books and produced critical essays relevant to their backgrounds—which program of study, grades or courses were taken were of minor consideration. Academic progress was considered.

Once in Japan students sent, initially by letter, lately by email, a monthly report on their progress and experiences. This communication was received by the president and members of the JEC. Personal growth, challenges faced and often homesickness were highly visible in the first few months. Towards the end of their stay students would report surprise at how fast the time had gone, how much they had learned about themselves and Japan and its people. The final letter usually described tearful farewells from their new friends and host families as well as from their teachers.

Capilano was fortunate that for 30 years Professor Nishio looked after our students, faculty and visitors. He taught Japanese History and Sociology, sometimes Kendo too, as well as serving *in loco parentis* to everybody from Capilano. One measure of the outstanding success of the Exchange is that no Capilano student ever failed to complete the program successfully. Obviously the committee and AG knew exactly what they were doing!

On the 25th anniversary of the exchange, to honour the work and commitment of Professor Nishio, Capilano held a special night, inviting back all previous students in the exchange, faculty in the exchange and JEC members. President Greg Lee thanked Nishio-san for his work and announced the creation of an endowed award called the Professor Nishio Award that would be used annually and in perpetuity to enhance the relationship between the two institutions.

Over the years many outstanding students have won the award. From a local CBC journalist to a Swiss-based Swarowski executive (who works daily in several languages), it has been enlightening to follow their careers. One such student is a young woman from Costa Rica who applied. The committee huddled over the idea of interviewing an ESL student and decided unanimously to treat all students equally. It was a wise decision. As that student left the interview we all realised we had just seen the winner of the year. Indeed, she earned an A+ in every course in Japan and a framed example of her writing in Kanji characters adorns the wall in the languages building at AG to this day. She returned to Japan on the JET program, ranked first among thousands in

Canada, and spent seven years advising school districts in Japan on English teaching methods and materials. She now resides in Alicante, Spain, teaching English and Spanish.

Another excellent student in her interview explained her interest in art and linked European Impressionism and contemporary Japanese art (she had done her homework and described a local village that did tie dyeing and another that made handmade paper from mulberry trees). Once in Japan she faced the challenge of a 9:00 p.m. curfew from her host father. She liked to go out dancing and wondered how this could be achieved without disobeying the power structure in which she was living. She learned that her host mother also loved dancing but the father did not. So she kindly "offered" to chaperone her mother to dancing evenings, and thus achieved a win-win for everybody. Her father commended her for her kindness. She graduated in Art History from U of T and now teaches ESL in Surrey.

We know some students came to Capilano expressly to apply for the AG exchange. One young woman came from Van Tech after a storied career in high school. When she won the award, the following day's assembly at Van Tech greeted the news with a thunderous ovation. This student was so integrated into her host family that the father started giving her his family name. When they stayed in hotels or registered anywhere she used the name—in short she achieved total integration and acceptance. She was delighted that she was treated exactly as a member of the family.

Of the male students there are many stories, but one stands out. He was in the Jazz Program and taught himself the first semester of Japanese and aced the second semester. Once in Aichi he established connections with jazz clubs in Nagoya.

After his formal studies were over, he worked in smoky cellars for several months playing piano. Upon his return to Canada he continued to study Japanese at UBC and ended up passing the highest level of exam in Japanese as a Second Language set by the national government.

As the success of the exchange became clear, the number of students was increased from 2 to 3, and male students were now eligible. The JEC continued to enjoy the full trust of the president and operated with total responsibility, authority and autonomy. Once Vice President Jim Cooke was asked to decide between two candidates when the JEC could not. Otherwise the administration accepted 100% every recommendation of every committee every year.

One of the hallmarks of the JEC was its longevity—the same team of members stayed together for almost 20 years. Barbara Hankin, who died tragically so soon after retiring, passed the Chair to Malcolm Fitz-Earle, who passed it on to me, and then I passed it on to Dorinda Neave, and all of us kept the operating principles and schedules virtually unchanged. The Dean of Developmental Education at Douglas College, himself a PhD in Japanese studies, expressed his envy of the exchange and explained he knew of no other equally successful and equally longstanding program in Canada.

So for students of both nations, faculty of both institutions and JEC members, the experience has been truly rewarding, and in many cases life-changing. The ongoing support of Capilano presidents has been a key factor throughout.

So what of the future? Well, Capilano College has become Capilano University, and Aichi Gakusen College, in Okazaki, has a sister institution, Aichi Gakusen University in Toyota City. This huge campus, beside a golf course and a shrine decorated with a full-sized statue of a white horse, boasts one of the top women's basketball teams in Japan. It also has a huge English component in its business program. Will we see exchanges of visiting sports teams or an integration of English / Business Studies in the future?

That future, building on the trust and mutual respect carefully nurtured over three decades by dedicated faculty experts in international education, is ripe with possibilities. It is our sincere hope that Capilano University in the future will continue to build on the exchange's past successes and strengthen even more the ties of this unique cultural exchange program.

THE START OF WOMEN'S STUDIES AT CAPILANO COLLEGE

JEAN CLIFFORD

"Never doubt that a small group of thoughtful
committed citizens can change the world;
indeed, it's the only thing that really has."

—MARGARET MEADE

On Monday, October 22, 1973, five young women aged 22 to 32—Penny LeCouteur (Sciences), Wanda Tilley (Careers), Karin Lind (Social Sciences), Sheila Perret (student), and I, Jean Clifford (Humanities)—piled into Wanda Tilley's recently purchased second-hand Fleetwood Cadillac, sandy gold with power steering, and headed out to catch the ferry to Victoria.

We felt nervous and anticipatory as Wanda drove us towards the legislature buildings for a morning meeting with Eileen Dailly, Minister of Education, to convince her of the need for a Women's Resource Centre and a series of outreach programs for women at Capilano. We came armed with a proposal whose rationale, "to investigate our lives and the cultural attitudes and political institutions that shape them," reflected the wider impact of rising feminism at that time.

With five key objectives, a Resource Centre, a Career Aims program to help women get back to work, a Community Education lecture series, academic credit courses, and liaisons with North Shore community women in mind, we each planned to speak our small piece.

Sheila, the youngest, recalls feeling intimidated, not by the government honchos, "but by my fellow travelers. Here I was in the company of all these academic brains. It was exhilarating and inspiring to be there with all of you." The rest of us, naïve, confident, and passionate, self-assuredly assumed that our cause would be heard.

Wanda Tilley, a strong NDP supporter, knew Hartley Dent, then Deputy Speaker of the house, and he had arranged for this meeting. After the meeting, Dailly invited us to lunch in the legislature's dining hall, and there, while we were eating "delicious clam chowder" (Wanda) and BC MacIntosh apples (Penny), Dave Barrett wandered by, curious about who we all were. Wanda introduced us, and Penny recalls choking a bit on her apple, overawed at being introduced to the premier.

He joked with us and then invited us to attend the caucus meeting that very afternoon to further present our proposal. A place at the caucus table was not something any of us had imagined or expected; however, we rallied from our great surprise. "We didn't know we were going to address caucus," says Karin. "At that point, I didn't even know what a caucus was."

However, Karin remembers the caucus table in detail—a long rectangular table where all five of us sat on one side, with Rosemary Brown, an elected MLA, sitting opposite us, nodding her encouragement as each of us got up to present our piece. Sheila, 22, remembers being "like a deer in the headlights," particularly when a few ministers in the caucus expressed amused skepticism.

"We all spoke enthusiastically, passionately and somewhat naïvely," says Karin. At one point, Rosemary Brown stood up, fluffed herself out, looked around and spoke. She inspired absolute silence. "Every time she opened her mouth, she said grand things," says Karin. Rosemary spoke vehemently in favour of our proposal. "I think we quite impressed them," remembers Penny.

At the end of the meeting, we thanked them for listening, and just got up and left. No promises had been made. A little subdued and tired, we headed back for the ferry, and discovered that Colin Gabelmann, MLA for North Vancouver-Seymour, was also on board. He joined us and spoke favourably about our proposal.

A few weeks later, we learned that Eileen Dailly had granted us seed money, $5000 in total, to organize ourselves for the following fall (1974–75). Certain conditions were attached—we needed to show a strong connection with the community, particularly with the North Shore Women's Centre which was in the process of creating itself; we needed to hire a coordinator, and we needed a clear program in place for the 1974 fall session. If these conditions were met, we would eventually receive $70,000 for operating costs.

Student Sheila Perret recalls being in the cafeteria pit on the new Lynnmour campus when someone shouted down the news that the money had come through. "Incredible," she remembers thinking, "incredible."

Incredulous was the more typical reaction of our administration and the College Board. Here this group of young women had bypassed the entire operating structure of the College (albeit a relatively new structure only a few years old), had bypassed the usual means of receiving money within the operating budget, and had, out of nowhere it appeared to them, gone and argued for a potential entity they were not at all sure they wanted.

Harold Kirchner, Dean of Careers, came on board with the

project fairly quickly as he was used to working with Wanda Tilley as the Administrative Science and Office Technology Coordinator. He was accustomed to the principle of spontaneity in the creation of fresh new courses that would appeal to students. Such career courses did not need university transfer status.

Doug Jardine, the brand-new Academic Dean, was inclined to the principle of academic autonomy within the system; however, he was initially skeptical about how all of this was going to work practically. His friendship with Penny LeCouteur added credibility to our proposal. "There was nothing in the rules that said we couldn't go to Victoria," Karin Lind says, "so we just did. I don't remember asking for the blessing of the administration before we went."

The most incredulous of all would have to have been the principal of Capilano at the time, Alf Glenesk. He and the Bursar of the College, Klaus Thiel, were completely confounded. At a Council meeting on November 5, where the money was initially announced, Diane Baigent, a brand-new NDP appointee to the Council, moved that "we accept with gratitude the offer of monies to fund a women's studies program." At that meeting, Glenesk "expressed surprise that the Minister granted money in such a manner," and "amazement that the agents of the Ministry were unaware of the College's priorities."

After the Council was reassured that these monies were a special grant which would not reduce other College monies, the motion passed, but Glenesk's antagonism did not. Clearly, a women's studies initiative was not one of his priorities.

Over the next spring months, two community women organized a conference attended by over 250 North Shore women (one of them was Andrea Kiss, who eventually worked in Wanda

Tilley's program). They were helped in this undertaking by Joy Smith, the Community Education Coordinator at Capilano College. This conference met the first requirement for the seed money, that connection be made with the North Shore Women's Centre, which had already developed an independent identity of its own.

At the same time, another internal Capilano group, the Women's Action Committee, was at work imagining the future for academic courses and workshops. They recommended working with Shelagh Day, a feminist activist in Vancouver, for the June / July period before the fall of 1974 to create workshop offerings appropriate to a Women's Resource Centre in preparation for hiring a coordinator in the fall.

A third group created a Women's Steering Committee, a group of ten, made up of six college women—two staff (Ann Gilbert and Shirley Freund), two faculty (Frances Brownell, then Burstein, and Wanda Tilley), two students (Andrea Lugsdin and Sheila Perret) and four community members. This group was to serve as a guiding body for the Resource Centre. The College Council, in fact, appointed Sheila Perret as the student representative, and she along with her cousin Andrea Lugsdin both participated. The Women's Steering committee began interviews to hire a coordinator for the fall.

By summer 1974, Alf Glenesk was beyond irritated. In early August, he and Thiel were suggesting that the arrangement was unworkable, that the women's program might better separate from the College entirely, that the $5000 paid out had gone through a "parallel bank account," that this money had needed to be within College funding within the main budget.

"We were made to feel like criminals," remembers Joy Smith,

"as if we were embezzling money." At a Board meeting on August 3, 1974, whose minutes are currently available from an old storage box, Glenesk reported that the women's group had applied for a grant and the minister had declined. Written over the notes of this board meeting by hand is the word WRONG in capital letters.

Peace between the administration and the operating Women's Steering Committee looked unlikely. The need to hire a coordinator, to define her relationship with the College as a consultant or an employee, and to establish her office space all needed to be resolved quickly or the larger operating funds would be lost.

Enter Harold Kirchner and Klaus Thiel. On August 28, 1974, they met with the ten-person Women's Steering Committee at a member's home to address the serious questions about the relationship between the College and this group. Mr. Thiel appeased the group by concluding that "there must have been some incorrect information referring to the bank account." One point settled.

Thiel then insisted that any further money received must be placed within the current operating budget of the College if the Steering Committee wanted the Women's Resource Centre Coordinator to be an employee and to get benefits. The Steering Committee reluctantly conceded, offering up a job description. Thiel stated that with that job description an employer-employee College relationship was now established.

Over the next few years, the Steering Committee met weekly, often at members' homes, and minutes of their very intensive meetings have been saved. In the year 1974–1975, they hired Kathy Stewart as the first Women's Centre Coordinator, and she was housed near Wanda Tilley in the C portable. "She was not thrilled with sharing an office in that cramped space," says Wanda.

Stewart left in a year and a half, citing in her resignation letter a cumbersome relationship with the Steering Committee (too many bosses) and an awkward job description with responsibility but no clear authority. She cited the conflict between the Steering Committee and the administration as a major cause of concern.

By December 1976 a new coordinator, Marsha Trew, with a much approved PhD was hired. Things settled down. Marsha Trew remained coordinator until the demise of the Centre and she, along with her wonderful assistant, Rita Johnson, created many workshops, working initially out of the posh office in Arbutus 108 originally designed for the new principal, Peter Spratt. When he didn't want it, they jumped at the chance for the space. Eventually, they moved into the M portable, closer to Counselling. With Marsha Trew's arrival, the Centre's identity became fully established.

To suggest that the flurry created by the group of five who headed to Victoria was a magical beginning for all this would be inaccurate, however. The lead-up to that Victoria event actually took place two years earlier.

In 1971–72, Wanda Tilley initiated weekly lectures called the Exploration series, offered to, for and by North Shore women. Women of all ages met in the West Vancouver High School cafeteria, where Capilano had begun its existence in a portable attached to the high school building.

Topics such as Fear of Success, Women and Corporate Capitalism, Indian Women Tell Their Story, and Marriage, Divorce and Custody show the variety and extent of this series.

The group of women who met and connected over this weekly series wanted to continue together the next year, says Carol McQuarrie, who attended them. In fact, they were so inspired by this series that they went on to create a series of their own.

They established an identity as the North Shore Women's Centre. Initially, they had no actual place to meet, so in 1972–73, they arranged to meet at North Shore Neighbourhood House, establishing another series of regular speakers, and among these was Rosemary Brown. Therefore, Rosemary Brown was possibly aware of this other group when we arrived in Victoria in 1973, and most likely for this reason, the seed funding was linked back to connecting with community women.

The Exploration series led to the formation of our group, says McQuarrie. "We were a spin off; we just wanted to keep on going. We had beer nights, meetings at Neighbourhood House." When community members were needed for the ten-person Steering Committee at Capilano College, they came directly from this group.

The North Shore Women's Centre became its own successful organization and has just celebrated its fortieth anniversary. It has worked to resolve social issues on the North Shore, creating Emily Murphy House, now Sage House, which aids battered women.

The relationship with Capilano College soon faded, says McQuarrie, as this group's initiatives and interests shifted towards more direct social action. However, two small links remain with Capilano in the form of awards. The North Shore Women's Centre Award goes each year to a mature woman returning to school. The Centre also involved itself initially with the Rita Watson Johnson award, given in memory of Rita

Johnson whose warm presence was much missed at the Women's Centre after her death. The Centre eventually transferred responsibility for this award back to the College, and, currently, it rests in Humanities where each year it provides funds for a woman beginning her studies.

But back to beginnings. While the Women's Steering Committee was active working on the Resource Centre, the Women's Action Committee was dreaming up academic course possibilities. Initially, from 1972–74, a number of us went back to our own departments to convince our colleagues to let us teach courses within the blanket of our own disciplines with a strong women's studies emphasis. Such courses would continue to be accredited as Psychology, Anthropology, History and English, but their content would be focused on women.

By the mid-1970s, however, things had shifted, as Simon Fraser began an accredited Women's Studies program and UBC began to grant General Studies credit for Women's Studies courses. "We began our push for a separate department," says Sandra Moe, who remembers Karin Lind's delight at getting a Xerox key with Women's Studies designation. "Once you've got a Xerox key, you're a department," she remembers Karin saying.

"We began creating outlines and calendar descriptions in the mid-seventies," says Sandra Moe, who joined Cap in January 1974. "That's when the first articulation for academic Women's Studies was beginning." To add further credibility, at one point we hosted a Women's Studies academic conference at Capilano, and all of us put on workshops. The guest speaker, UBC's Annette Kolodny, gave a rousing speech in the cafeteria pit. Once we had hosted the conference, we were part of the Women's Studies system.

Just a brief sideline into the fall of 1974. This was, I believe, the first year for the 4 × 4 system, when the maximum workload was four courses meeting four hours per week, down from five courses. Thus we had a major influx of new hirings, and a number of these hirings were women. Many of them went on to become willing participants in women's issues.

That was also the year that I personally received an unpaid leave for two years to begin my PhD studies back east, so that by the time I arrived back on campus two years later, the academic Women's Studies courses were already in full process. Sandra Moe wrote her first Psychology of Women outline in 1975; Marlene Legates had already conceived and initiated the introductory 100-level Women's Studies overview course, which she taught for a number of years. Penny LeCouteur recalls teaching a couple of sessions of Women in Science, as does Karin for Anthropology.

In the fall of 1976, on my return, the academic committee encouraged me to teach a course on Canadian Women Writers, which is probably in the top ten of my all-time favorite courses to teach. Just before I left to begin my PhD in 1974, I was called into Principal Glenesk's office. His parting words to me were: "Pride goeth before the fall."

The Women's Studies program did fall on hard times in the early 1980s when cuts swept though the College. Sandra Moe remembers begging Frank Gelin, the academic Dean at the time, to at least keep the courses listed in the College calendar.

The designation, "not offered this year," appeared under a number of listings. Since these early beginnings, the Women's Studies program has engaged many enthusiastic instructors who have continued to bring their passion and energy to these courses.

Two other of the original mandates presented in Victoria

proved less cumbersome to realize. Wanda Tilley initiated the Career Alternatives program for women transitioning back into the workforce.

"This was an intensive sixteen-week five-day-a-week program," says Carol McCandless, one of the later instructors along with Andrea Kiss and Yetta Lees who worked in this program for a number of years.

"Can you imagine this program happening now?" Carol McCandless asked. "So much money went into this initiative." Joy Smith continued to produce non-credit courses specifically geared to women's needs throughout the 70s, responding very quickly to community requests. She worked with both the Counselling Department and Marsha Trew in the Resource Centre on many initiatives. Wanda Tilley also recalls a course they created on women in power. Notable women in power such as Diana Davidson, the lawyer, taught this course.

This piece speaks only to beginnings, but I must say, I am glad I was there. So many women, so much synergy, so much energy, so much fun, even some interesting and powerful conflicts. Deep friendships have continued to flourish between individual women who worked closely together on many committees for this cause.

Thank you to Wanda Tilley, Karin Lind, Sheila Perret, Penny LeCouteur, Joy Smith, Carol McCandless, Carol McQuarrie, Andrea Kiss and Sandra Moe for their willingness to drive down memory lane with me. Thank you to Trevor Smith, the reference librarian, who managed to locate early files handed over by Frances Brownell (Burstein) whose handwritten WRONG still covers one page. My apologies to the many women who were also active during this time whose names I have inadvertently missed. Karin Lind asked that I preface this piece with Margaret Meade's quotation, and indeed, it does capture the feeling this experience gave to everyone involved.

MEMORIES OF THE CAPILANO COLLEGE MUSIC DEPARTMENT, 1969–1974

JOYCE GEE

THE YEARS 1969 TO 1974 were pivotal years in my life. These were my years as a student in the Capilano College Music department. These were the years that changed my perception of what was possible for me.

My association with Capilano College began in 1968. I was a single mother of two children, eking out a living teaching piano lessons. My kids were in school, my piano teaching job began at 3:30 p.m., and I was looking for something between the hours of 9 a.m. and 3 p.m. that would enhance my life beyond working for a living and raising kids.

I had had, for as long as I can remember, a passion for history. When I discovered that there was a college just a mile from my home (Capilano College was operating out of St. David's Church at Taylor Way and the Upper Levels Highway), and that part-time students of all ages were welcome, I signed up for a European History course. The instructor was dedicated and he was excellent; I participated, did well, and was hooked. I then enrolled in a Canadian History course, and had the same experience.

On my way to my Canadian History course one day, I noticed a Music Theory course run by Ken Perry. I peered in and saw that a number of my private music instructor colleagues were enrolled in this course; I also subsequently enrolled. Like my colleagues, I had studied music theory as a child and therefore knew a lot of the material being covered. But revisiting this material as an adult with a practical teaching background turned out to be an exhilarating experience.

Mr. Perry structured his course according to the prior learning level of the vast majority of his students, and he certainly challenged us. For our final exam, we wrote string quartets! Most if not all of us were pianists, and we were also required to reduce our compositions to short scores and play them in class on the piano.

One day, we had a substitute teacher who was completing a master's degree in Music Composition at UBC His name was Karl Kobylansky. He was challenging, provocative, and somewhat frightening all at the same time.

The next year, Karl was hired by Capilano College to teach music. At the time the job consisted of one course in music theory. However, Karl was able to expand the music offerings: new faculty were hired, notably Linda Falls, a piano performance specialist with an MMus. in Piano Performance, and Anita Sleeman, a UBC master's degree candidate in Music Composition. Thus began the fledgling program which would eventually become the Music department at Capilano College.

These were heady and experimentally exhilarating years. As coordinator of the Music department, Karl Kobylansky had a long-range plan to establish a two-year music program transferable to UBC But in the meantime he had to provide courses for the existing student population. Most of us were private music teachers with a more or less two-year university equivalent of music theory, and a passable level of performance skills. However, there were also some very young students who had little if any formal music training but great performance skills. The faculty's job was to develop courses that would serve the current eclectic group of students enrolled in music, in order to hang on to the section allocation that had been negotiated. Among those courses:

1. 20th Century Music Theory. None of the potential student population at Capilano College at that time knew much if anything about 20th century music. Aspects of that music, like Dodecaphony and Indeterminacy, did not necessarily require a "traditional" music background. These 20th century music trends became the nucleus of a theory course where students of varying backgrounds in music were enrolled on a more or less level playing field:

    a) Students with a substantial music background in 18th century music (most had ARCT Diplomas from the Toronto Conservatory of Music) wrote 12-tone compositions, and compositions focussing on the principles of Indeterminacy. Though we complained a lot, we did theory projects that I now realize would have been respectable projects at a graduate level.

    b) Students with no theoretical music background were also able to write 12-tone and compositions based on the principles of Indeterminacy, and in the case of Indeterminacy, appeared to be more comfortable than we trained musicians, because they could improvise and were used to performing.

    c) Theory students were required to perform their creations for each other. We had to negotiate amongst ourselves for performers willing to learn and perform another colleague's composition. It ultimately made for a spirit of co-operation rather than competition.

2. Medieval Music Theory / History. This was another area where students had little or no background. Starting with simple Gregorian chants we learned how four-part harmonic music evolved over the centuries. The course was taught by Anita Sleeman, who was a composer. Anita didn't distinguish between music history and theory. Her theory courses always had a strong historical context, and her history courses usually involved some creative project.

   In one course, we were given a Gregorian chant and assigned the writing of a Medieval Motet for the purpose of learning, in a practical way, how music grew from a single line of music to the four-part harmony we were familiar with, and we were required to have these compositions performed in class by our classmates. Though it took a great deal of time (particularly the rounding up of a trio to learn and perform your composition), it was in the end a bonding experience.

3. Piano Repertoire. Linda Falls developed and taught this course. Originally we were a small class of students, mostly over the age of 30, most of us teaching piano privately, but who were not performing publicly. Music repertoire was drawn from the Renaissance to the 20th century. We were required to learn and perform the music. We learned performance practices—I didn't know at the time that improvisation was big in the Baroque period, and that the notation of this period was to some degree meant to act as a guideline. To the extent it was possible and practical, we performed on period instruments. One year the College brought in a harpsichord. This course was a great practical history lesson, it was immensely helpful to me as a piano teacher, and it got me playing the piano publicly again.

The course took off and soon we were joined by singers and instrumentalists, all of whom needed piano accompanists.

4. Ensemble: Though Capilano College already had a community choir, a small ensemble called Music Collegium was added to the list of departmental offerings. The ensemble was dedicated to the music of the Renaissance. The leader of the ensemble, Karl Kobylansky, was never known for doing anything halfway. Before we knew it we had authentic Renaissance instruments, and costumes to boot. We even performed Renaissance dances.

There were some very funny times.

One in particularly comes to mind: The music faculty used to put on skits for the students at the end of term. One year they did *Swan Lake*. The faculty were all dressed up in tutus, with Karl as the Black Swan. Just nearing the end of their performance, the Dean, Harold Kirchner (having got wind of this performance), summoned the music faculty to his office immediately. They all trooped over to Kirchner's office in their tutus.

By the time I transferred to the UBC Music department, in 1974, the music department at Capilano College had evolved into a full two-year transfer program, with a profile that resembles that of the current Bachelor of Music Transfer Program. Some of the early eclectic courses had to be abandoned to accommodate a more traditional two-year music profile.

In 1978, I was hired to teach a music history course at Capilano College. Thus began my career as an instructor in the Music department. By this time the department had expanded to include two other programs—Music Therapy and Commercial Music.

When I retired in 2001, Capilano College had three distinct music programs: A two-year transfer program—Bachelor of Music Transfer Program—and two four-year degree programs, Jazz Studies and Music Therapy.

Though I have many treasured memories of my association with Capilano College, the years 1969 to 1974, when I was a student in the Music department, were pivotal years for me, that fundamentally changed the direction of my life. In 1969 I didn't really know the significance that music might play in my life. I only knew that I was a piano player who had qualifications to teach piano.

These were difficult years for young instructors trying to forge a program with an eclectic bunch of part-time students of various ages, with varying levels of training and experience. But through their ingenuity, commitment and dedication they did it! The sheer creativity of the course offerings themselves taught me how little I knew and made me want to know more. The encouragement of the music faculty helped to give me the confidence to go on with music studies.

In 1974, I had transferred to UBC with a view to hopefully working in music at a college or university level. This began a potentially significant change of direction in my life. It came to fruition in 1978 when I was appointed as an instructor in the Capilano College Music department—a position I held until retiring in 2001.

The cafeteria and Pit also served as
a registration area in the 1970s.

The Pit was a feature of the Library building
in the 1970s: A cafeteria with a sunken area for
meetings, performances, and hanging out.

LESSONS LEARNED AT CAPILANO COLLEGE

DOUGLAS K. JARDINE

This memoir is part of a longer autobiographical work by Dr. Jardine. After describing his early life in Guyana and then settling in Canada, he explains his decision to leave Mount Royal College in 1972. We begin his narrative at this point.

THE FIRST EXIT I explored was the presidency of Selkirk College. I was short listed, interviewed, but not hired. Instead, the Board hired an American who, as I recall, lasted less than two years—a foreshadowing of my future experiences in presidential searches at Cap. My second exit opportunity arose when Mike McNeil wrote to me saying that I should apply for new position of Dean of Academic Studies at Cap (he and I had worked together at Mount Royal before he left to join Cap).

I applied, was interviewed (Penny LeCouteur and Rick Salter were two people I remember being on the search committee), was hired, and began work on July 1, 1972. I was often in my (famous) thick green cardigan / sweater, no tie, no jacket, a practice that got under the skin of Alf Glenesk, the College's founding principal, who suggested that I should dress like a dean. He wasn't happy with my answer which was to the effect that in my limited experience what I wore did not seem to either improve or degrade my capacity to think clearly.

However, it wasn't long before I caused my first real controversy. Sonja Sanguinetti, chair of Social Sciences, presented me a short list of candidates to interview. I interviewed them and recommended that the College hire Ed Lavalle. I had chosen Ed over another candidate with, as I recall, a PhD and SFU experience.

This unsuccessful candidate took the matter to the union, declaring that I had asked some most unusual questions for an interview for an academic position. The union chose not to support his case after which Rick Salter and Art Pape came by my office to tell me about the situation. They told me that their reply to the argument based on my asking unusual questions was that they were not surprised since their dean was an unusual man in whom they had complete confidence.

During my twenty-three years at Cap I never once regretted my decision to recommend that Ed be hired. He was always every bit the teacher that represented the standard of teaching that I, as dean or president, wanted for Cap.

If I recall correctly the dates and timelines, Alf Glenesk resigned in 1974. I applied to fill the vacant position. I was shortlisted and the process allowed Board members to interview these candidates privately if they cared to, in addition to the formal interviews. One Board member chose to interview me privately and at the end of a pleasant, polite and probing interview he told me that he would not vote in favour of my candidacy. His reasons, he explained, had to do with his judgment that I was too much of a "faculty administrator"; he didn't think I could or would properly explain and implement the tough decisions the Board might need to take against faculty.

The Board's decision was to hire Peter Spratt, a college educator from Ontario. About eighteen months later, the Board passed a resolution terminating Spratt and then asked me to take up the position of acting principal, which I did. I was happy to do this, not because I saw it as a step up on the ladder of my career, but because the College had become embroiled in difficult circumstances, not least of which was that it was getting too many column inches in the Hansard of the provincial legislature over Spratt issues, and I believed I had the skills to reestablish the institution's lost normalcy. I figured that if I could "fix" Mount Royal, Cap shouldn't be all that difficult.

Soon after my acting appointment was made public, Rick Salter and Art Pape paid me another visit in my office, this time to explain the faculty union's pending action. We're here, they said, to let you know in advance that the union is going to file a grievance over your appointment. We're also here to explain and assure you that the union has no issue with you being the acting principal for we believe you are qualified to do the job with one hand tied behind your back. However, we must file this grievance because the Board has breached its obligation to consult with us on the appointment of anyone to this position.

I thanked them for the courtesy and made a mental note to myself that my first teachable moment with the Board was about to unfold: it had to do first with collegiality, and second with the obligation of a party to a contract to honour both the spirit and the language of the contract. The grievance was resolved, but I forget the details of the resolution.

My first College budget included the termination of two senior administrative positions, the dean of student services and the dean of community education; beyond that I can't recall any details, yet I am sure that there were other cuts involved.

The public meeting at which the Board's finance committee would present the budget for adoption was held at the West Vancouver School Board offices. The chair of the finance committee was a West Van trustee and he moved adoption of the budget as tabled. There was discussion after which the question was called. I experienced a certain sense of dismay as I watched the chair of the finance committee raise his hand as not in favour of the motion. As my surprise wore off, I realised I had just been schooled for the first time in the arena of local politics, posturing and grandstanding. The budget passed and I lost the dean of student services as a friend.

I went on to serve sixteen months as acting principal, after which Paul Gallagher was appointed as president. For that search I was not an applicant and at no time did I ever give any thought to applying to be the college's third president; the role of dean of academic studies still held much excitement for me. I do recall, still with some amusement, one of the short-listed candidates (before Paul was even an applicant for the position) withdrew his application after his meeting with the faculty association.

Ahead of the search process, I had committed to the Board that I would answer each candidate's questions of me in a full-disclosure mode—no gilding the lily on any topic. As he and I drove back from our lunch together, en route to his meeting with the association, he asked what he might expect. I told him to be sure that he had his jock strap securely in place because my guess was that it would be like no other experience he'd ever had before. He had no sense of humour and simply looked at me with a sour expression.

In short order Gallagher restructured the senior instructional administration. He asked me to take on the position of dean of student and instructional services, which I did assuming that he had learned enough about me to be confident that I could do the job. I accepted the reassignment and must report that Salter and Pape did not pay a visit to my office, although they may have visited Paul in his office—don't know and never did ask. Frank Gelin was hired as the new Dean of Academic Studies and Harold Kirchner was the Dean of Career Programs.

I was named as the permanent chair of what became known as the Committee of Deans to most, but the Group of Deans (or GOD) by others, and we were given T-shirts so decorated. Harold left to go to Camosun College and Greg, appointed as the dean to replace Harold, became a member of the CoD. To be clear, Paul's charge to the CoD was that we, as a committee, shall manage and be responsible for everything within this organization that has to do with students and the teaching and learning environment.

Outside of Cap we were often referred to as the Capilano mafia. We were three peas in a pod: a chemist who had studied statistics applied to psychology, an engineer who had studied physical chemistry, and a physicist who had stuck to physics. Together, we had a remarkably good five-cent bullshit filter that operated both inside and outside of the College. It was not often that we would be fooled by a presentation, not often that we would miss an opportunity, not often that we would back down in the face of pressures from a university or from the ministry responsible for advanced education in the province. In short, we were a force to be reckoned with.

Paul assigned all three of his deans additional responsibilities as necessary. For almost every set of negotiations during his term, he assigned me to be the chief negotiator on behalf of the Board. It was not an assignment I ever went looking for; not one for which I had any basis to refuse; not one that I relished in any way.

Looking back on my years at Cap, even including the assignment to lead the employer's side of the negotiations, I can say without hesitation that, all things considered, the CoD years were the best years of my career at Capilano. Greg who followed me as president says the same thing. There is just something about the presidency that is different, more wearing, more isolating; it's all that, and more, when you accept personal responsibility for the way the institution is managed.

I suppose it was inevitable in 1985 when Paul left for Vancouver Community College, that I would once again be asked to serve as acting principal. I was asked, and I accepted the assignment, knowing that I would not be an applicant for the position.

Almost every week the then Chair of the Board, Hilda Rizun, would ask me if I had applied, and after I said I had not, she would go through the routine of you should, I would like you to, please do it. (I guess here is as good a spot as any to say that as a principal of some kind or as president, I served under Board chairs Graham Crockart, Nancy Farley, Jim MacDonald, Norris Martin, Hilda Rizun, and Robin Wilson.)

Finally, just before the deadline for submitting an application I succumbed to the Rizun good-natured nagging. In my interviews in the 1974 search, my argument on my behalf had been simply that my management skills were sufficient for the job; that I understood collegiality and practiced it as the Dean of Academic Studies. I don't recall offering any vision of the institution's future under my leadership. In short, I now readily admit that I could not possibly have been the best candidate that the Board interviewed in 1974.

But in January 1986 when the interviews were held, it was a different Doug that stood up in a public setting chaired by Norris Martin, the chair of the Board's search committee, to say that the province deserved a "Harvard of the North" in the BC college system and that Capilano College ought to be that Harvard of the North, and that that was my vision for the College. As the saying goes, that set the cat among the pigeons. Why would a straight-shooting engineer / scientist speak in metaphors? He must mean the death of everything other than his beloved academic studies. It was of course a metaphor for the College to be the best, beyond dispute, at everything it did.

Once again, I came in second. I was plain spoken, reliable, dependable, intelligent, thoughtful, could manage people and situations, and had the PhD. My guess is that the winner had all of those qualities plus a raft of publications, experience at a much bigger institution, experience with a much larger budget, and no doubt far fewer rough edges than I did, which is the intangible I think we call charisma.

Years later on a visit to the University of Calgary where he was the president, I introduced myself to him as the man who had come in second to him at Capilano College. He was momentarily taken aback, but we did enjoy a brief conversation. He had turned down the offer of employment, probably for technical reasons under the rubric of terms and conditions of employment, but my guess is that he realized that a term as principal, perhaps changed later to president, was not going to move him towards the presidency of a respectable national university.

The truth is that I slid in to the position through the back door. Early on in my appointment I would say to questioners that I was not the Board's first choice, but like Avis, as number two I intended to try harder.

So, did I have goals and did I achieve them? The answer to the first part is "yes," and to the second it is "some," perhaps "most." However, my trepidation is that while the events that I write about did undoubtedly occur, the timing and the sequence I declare herein may well be wrong and the related circumstances and processes may not be as I describe them; I am particularly sensitive to this possibility when I write about my presidency.

And why might this be so? Because when a task or job or event or crisis is over, I quickly forget the details and move on to the next "adventure." My memory of those years has definitely faded and all that I have that might refresh it is about 12 inches of paper (in three manila file folders)—that is my total collection of papers, documents and the like that is the detritus of my twenty-three years at Cap.

They have helped remind me of some of the "big items" that I had on my mind during my presidency—there were undoubtedly other big items but I simply don't recall them, although I might if an interviewer were to prompt me.

My primary all-encompassing goal was my vision for the College to be a Harvard of the North. But what, in today's leadership language, were the core strategies and critical success factors that would get us, the organization, to that point? And further, since "Harvard of the North" was seen by some, perhaps many, as a divisive statement of intent rather than a vision for the character of the College, I needed a substitute "bumper sticker." If you can't print your corporate vision on a sticker that you can place on the bumper of your car (like BMW's "*the ultimate driving machine*," unchanged for years), you don't yet have a vision for your corporation. It is simply not possible for the people of the corporation to rally round a paragraph of rhetoric.

I realized that "Harvard of the North" could never be that bumper sticker: it's arrogant on the one hand and on the other it reeks of "wannabe"; but more importantly, it would be impossible to align the College's employees in support of a phrase that was not immediately self-evident.

However, it served its purpose: it got people arguing, debating, and best of all thinking, and that last is what I wanted the people of the College to be known as and for—thoughtful people dedicated to an attainable vision for the College, i.e., the future we wanted to create for the College.

As I recall I had instituted an institution-wide planning process not long after I was named president. I don't remember exactly when it was, or what the process was, or who were the key participants to the process. I don't have in my files a copy of the final report or the plan or any other documentation related to the process. But the old hands of the College will remember the result: "*Capilano College—your first choice.*" This was a bumper sticker whose meaning and intent were immediately self-evident.

By God, if we were going to be an institution of first choice, we would have to be damn good; damn good at everything we put our hand to. It doesn't need a paragraph of rhetoric (that too many people think of, incorrectly, as a mission statement) to say that the bumper sticker meant that our instructors and staff are going to be the best, our curriculum the best, our support services the best, our management and governance practices the best, our graduates the best. These are the details that you spell out in the "business concept" as an elaboration of the mission statement.

(I should add here as an aside that during my years as president I became increasingly interested in the theory and practice of strategy as distinct from the theory and practice of management, and governance, especially corporate governance. I read these topics—sort of like going to Oxford to read chemistry—carefully and intensely, which led to my post-retirement activities of "consulting on issues of strategy, management and governance." That turned out to be a great gig involving work with Boards and their senior managers to craft strategic plans and how to lead the consequential change within their organizations. However, that's another story.)

The goals, those core strategies for a successful "institution of first choice" immediately became apparent to me. What I now describe is my "thinking back" construct of a set of core strategies and critical success factors, as a sort of amalgam of my ideas over nine years of my presidency, that I think are a faithful rendition of what I would have had on my mind during those years. They are, in no particular order other than the first had to be the first among equals, as follows:

1. I would have to find ways and means by which the Board and management would choose to remake the everyday professional and operational relationships with the unions, particularly the CCFA, and more broadly faculty and staff as the people of the institution. My preference was to cooperate and be collegial; but ultimately, if the other party didn't want to play in that sandbox and would rather fight, I'd be ready to fight and I didn't back down from gladiators.

1.1 The most important critical success fact related to the CCFA and had to do with workload. I don't remember the timing of the workload negotiations. There were two of note: one in which the negotiated collective agreement changed the workload from 4 × 4 to 5 × 3 and later one which reinstated the 4 × 4 workload.

I don't want to deny the baggage I acquired from this issue, so given that my reply letter to a faculty member reminds me that there were settlements in '85, '86 and '88, my hand would have been on the move to 5 × 3, either as chief negotiator or as acting principal, or perhaps even as president, in either '85 or '86. What is important to me is that my hand as president was on the return to the 4 × 4 workload model, which must have been no later than '88.

1.2 A second critical success factor related to disclosure of information and more generally, communications. My views came out of my readings on "open book" management and the related idea of "servant leadership."

1.2.1 Specifically in terms of the College's relationships with the unions it meant that if either union had questions about budgets or expenditures, they should speak directly with the VP Finance (Marie Jessup), and that if they didn't think they were getting the straight goods from her, they should bring this to my attention and we'd go together to Marie's office to get the scoop. If there were questions of a non-financial nature, then visit the appropriate VP and the same rule applied: if you weren't satisfied, then get me and we'd go back together to the VP.

I can't recall ever being invited by a union representative to join him / her on a visit to a VP's office. The VPs understood that my expectation was that they would inform, for my belief was and is that if the employees don't understand they can't deliver their best for the institution.

1.2.2 For my part, I operated an open-door office; if my door was open, and most of the time when I was there it was open, anyone could knock and they would be invited in. No one had to run the gauntlet of the president's protector secretary. Barbara Boyce would see someone coming and say, if you want to see him, just knock and go on in (I sat with my back to the door).

A Business Management faculty member used to tell his / her class about this—he's accessible, go up with no appointment and check it out. I met a number of most surprised students that way.

1.2.3 I used to pick up hitch-hiking students leaving the College and chat with them about their life as a student at Cap. Some would engage in the "and who are you?" bit; Oh, I work for the College; "so, what do you teach"? Well, my discipline is chemistry. I would always answer their questions clearly at the end of the ride. Sometimes I'd hear good things and sometimes not so good things; I'd make a mental note of both and follow up either by asking innocent questions of my college colleagues, or if the "good" was extraordinary, by sending the employee one of my hand-written personal notes of thanks or congratulations. I never asked a student their name, and when I dropped them off, I always told them my name and my position at the College, and thanked them for the conversation.

1.2.4 Perhaps one other example is in order: my "from the President" letters. The letters, when they were not simply updates, were from my perspective evidence-based arguments in support of what I thought was the right thing for us to do about an issue of the moment. I don't have a collection of those letters, but if they are in an archive somewhere I'm sure we would find the Foundation and fundraising, pay parking, the Sportsplex, and labour relations issues, among the issues that I addressed.

1.2.5 Finally, the occasional all-College forums that I would arrange, particularly those on the annual budget I planned to recommend to the Board.

Some members of the Board were not happy with my all-college forums to address the budget. My draft budget for the Board's consideration was prepared using information and advice obtained through the operational meeting structure of the College. It also reflected what I thought that the Board would ultimately be willing to adopt; I kept them apprised of the contents of the developing budget and thus in fact my recommended budget never contained any surprises. (A management dictum is never let your boss be surprised.)

The unhappy Board members said that because employees were hearing my recommendations first, the Board was being framed into supporting their president. I said not so: first of all, my duty is to provide the Board with the best set of recommendations and to do so I needed to hear in a plenary type of setting the "good" and the "bad" of my draft budget from the people who did the real work of the College.

Second, I reminded the Board members that they had a fiduciary obligation to make decisions based on the evidence the president presented and whatever else they knew by whatever means. I explained that often the final decision would simply be one of several reasonable alternatives and that it was possible that in their opinion the president had not chosen the best alternative and hence they would in fact decide otherwise.

At its best, that's how the system should work: the Board should not be perceived as rubber-stamping the president's decisions nor should they in reality be rubber-stamping them. If the Board's decision was not one that I was recommending, they could depend on it that I would explain and defend their decision as persuasively as I could. The Board agreed that I could proceed with these budget forums, and for this I was glad since it helped us to avoid a return to the Board / union power struggles of old.

Of course this approach depends greatly on trust, and I like to think that I and my management team were trusted by both the Board and the unions.

2 I would have to find ways and means to put the community back into the warp and weft of the College's everyday activities as a community college.

2.1 For me the key critical success factor was that the College had to be seen as more than a collection of classrooms staffed by first-rate faculty, supported by dedicated staff, and indeed be all of that in reality. From a management perspective, this was not something that you planned; management simply had to give a blanket permission for employees to take part in community affairs as an exemplar of being a good citizen.

What I'm saying here is that if the people of the institution understood that this core strategy contributed to vision-attainment, and that in turn the critical success factor contributed to the effectiveness of the core strategy, then they could be safely left to use their imagination and good judgment regarding the best actions to contribute to us being a "first choice" institution. The only precaution to take would be to say what they could not do—and this is far easier to prescribe than trying to prescribe all the things they might do.

2.1.1 At the risk of leaving out some important contributors and their contributions, I recall Alan Smith working a process by which warring North Shore community arts councils learned to cooperate and achieve superior results for the arts communities of the North Shore. The process was later adopted and adapted for use elsewhere in the province by other organizations.

2.1.2 Dave Brewer was a leader on the North Shore Search and Rescue operations. I made sure that he knew that when the call came in that he was needed on the mountain, he was to make a decision: was the need on the mountain more important and valuable than the tasks he was working on at that moment? If it was, he needed no one's permission "to leave his desk" immediately, only that I expected him to do whatever it took to accomplish his tasks on their predetermined timeline.

2.1.3 Faculty and staff began working that extra measure as they became elected to various community boards or engaged in activities that supported the development of healthy communities.

2.1.4 There were a host of other activities that administrators, faculty and staff engaged in which all served to return the College to the status of a community college such as had not been seen since the inaugural days of the College. Even the president contributed by teaching the occasional "your friendly computer" course for Continuing Education.

3 A third core strategy would require the linking and combination of select "communication" and "community" critical success factors.

3.1 Club Optima was an example of this. Club Optima was our annual "see the campus, meet the faculty, and have a hot dog" event in the spring for Grade 12 high school students selected by their high schools at what we hoped would be their institution of first choice. Those who made it to hot dog time got the T-shirt as a reward. The timing was right around when those students would be deciding what post-secondary institution they would attend, if they intended to continue their education in the fall.

3.2 As president, I was on a speaking schedule developed by our communications and PR department. I spoke to parents' groups, to Rotary and Chamber of Commerce groups, and other groups such as the U of T Alumni group in Vancouver as an example.

My speaking engagements were not restricted to the North Shore. For parents, my story was about the institution of first choice that would welcome their children to our classrooms. For the Rotary and Chamber type audiences, the presentation was about those of our activities that linked with business and industry, making our graduates valuable to employers either upon graduation from Cap or after they had earned a university degree. For the more sophisticated audiences with wider interests, I spoke about the changes occurring in the economy and the need for change in the educational sector in terms of content and methodology, and what Cap was doing in an effort to keep in step with the changes in the business and social environment. I always went armed to the teeth with data and real-world examples.

All in all, this added to the newsworthy index of the College. The College was the talk of the North Shore, and elsewhere in Greater Vancouver. All this talk of first choice rankled some of my colleague presidents, to whom I replied that if they wanted to be first, they'd have to beat us, but if they didn't want to be first, then there was a lot of room for them in second place and below.

4 A fourth core strategy was one having to do with programs and services.

4.1 There were two critical success factors: one related to the continuous renewal of existing curricula and the second related to the development of new programs and services.

In the case of the first success factor, we were able to depend on the faculty to develop and tweak existing programs into improved versions, or spin off a variant. In the case of the second factor, two new programs really unlike anything else already at the College come to mind: Gerry Blitzstein and the InfoTech program, and the folks in the ABE area with the SARAW software enabling students with serious motor-skill and related impediments to communicate, often for the very first time.

4.2 There was a third critical success factor, and it had to do with the re-mandating of some colleges to university colleges; much later still came the re-mandating of university colleges to universities.

In 1988 some colleges were re-mandated as university colleges, but not Cap. I was very disappointed. I can recall contemplating the list and in a moment of pure and unadulterated corporate arrogance asking myself about one college on the list, how come that one and not us? Cap was at the time the academic college of the system and I just couldn't understand how or why we had not made the list. In retrospect, I guess this time I had been schooled in a different branch of politics and educational warfare fought at the provincial level. I think this would have to count among my failures: failure to keep my head up and see what was going on outside of Cap while I was focusing on developing Cap as a college of first choice and attending to getting matters inside Cap on an even keel.

As an executive we grappled with the question: what should Cap's response be in terms of either gaining university college status or gaining some alternative authority? By 1990, while we had not abandoned a watching brief for an opportunity to gain university college status, I was on the hustings promoting degree-granting status for the College. "New degrees for the new economy" was my tag line.

What I wanted was for Cap to remain a community college but now have the authority to grant a specific kind of degree, an "applied studies" degree. I said that the litmus test for any applied degree we proposed was a simple one: if it smacked of a degree already offered by SFU or UBC, then somehow we had made a dreadful mistake in our submission and we would stand ready to either withdraw the proposal or amend it to make it clearly unlike any traditional degree.

This was not an idle proposition, for during my acting principal days after Paul's departure we had developed a post-baccalaureate program. One of our counsellors (I can see him in my mind's eye but can't for the life of me call up his name) had an idea for a program that would admit students with a baccalaureate degree and prepare them for work in South East Asia and Japan (my memory may well be faulty on the geographic regions intended). The program would involve language, culture and management training plus a work-study period in the country for which the student was preparing to work. I was smitten by the idea and the program development work was done; the program was launched and it was a hit.

Interesting story here. When we applied for provincial government funding for this program, the ADM, Dr. Jack Newberry, said No, and by the way you have no business offering programs that require a degree for entrance. I said, Jack, I've read the fine print and there is nothing that stops us from setting that entrance requirement. Furthermore, we'll raise the money from other sources and we'll run the program. And, what's more, I'll be back and you will eventually fund this program.

We got the first funding from a federal government source through a grant application. That year we beat out applications from SFU and other universities—this in part I'm sure because I had retained as a consultant a person who had served as an adjudicator of those applications in previous years to critique our document until we got it right in his eyes. We did eventually get provincial government funding for the program.

In 1990 then, my notion was that we would develop other post-baccalaureate programs whose point was to make BA and BSc graduates more attractive to employers, and we would press hard for either degree-granting status as a college or re-mandating to a university college. Of the latter two, I preferred the former option.

But none of that happened on my watch. As I will address later, the squeeze on government funding to education, and perhaps the colleges in particular, had begun. Count that as a failure. Was I not up to the task? Perhaps; or was there somewhere in the Ministry a standing order of "nyet" to constrain that upstart Capilano? Paranoid, perhaps.

In 1994, at a time when everyone knew I was in my last months as president, I think it fair to say that it had become obvious to me that Cap was not going to gain entrée to the world of degrees during my time. That breakthrough would come, hopefully, on the next president's watch. However, there was an additional wrinkle in the offing. The university colleges were beginning to mount a full court press to be re-mandated yet again, this time to university status.

This allowed for discussion around the hypothetical question, Cap for university status, Yes or No? (Forgive me if here I am conflating issues that were post-Jardine with those that were before my retirement.)

The arguments pro and con on Cap as a university were manifold and obvious to most. There were good arguments to be made on either side of the question, particularly if you assumed in the hypothesis that there were no longer any alternatives from which to choose: it would be a college and university post-secondary system, plus of course the previously established institutes.

Frankly, I privately thought that the whole idea of Cap as a university was a strategic conceit. What a row to hoe, trying to be a university of consequence, a university in more than name only, when standing square in the shadow of SFU and UBC, on funding that I couldn't imagine would be increased to finance the true costs of what a CapU should be doing, not even as a teaching university.

Being close to the end of my tenure at Cap, I was careful to hold private this personal view and never spoke out against the proposition of university status for Cap. By November

1994, if I remember correctly, the Board had announced that Greg would be the next president and I had no desire to be an *eminence grise* making life difficult for him on important issues that were possibly in their earliest period of secret gestation. I suppose you could count all this as another failure of mine.

4.3 The fourth critical success factor had to do with delivering education on a contract basis. This was largely (perhaps entirely, I can't remember) contract training funded directly by the federal government.

Here we had to very careful not to lose our shirts. The Feds didn't want to fund for anything more than the direct cost of training, but they demanded an inordinate amount of reporting and other duties that tended to push us beyond what we felt was a reasonable contribution from our other revenues. Marie Jessup was a skilled bargainer with their representatives, and once we had begun to say "no" to them on some of their proposed purchases, i.e., they could keep their money, they became a bit more reasonable.

5 A fifth core strategy had to do with the then-moribund Capilano Foundation and the whole matter of fundraising through an Office of Resource Development.

The board of the Foundation was then made up of long-time friends of the College, friends from the inaugural days of the College. Initially they were fearful that my approach to reinvigorate the Foundation was simply a scheme for the College to take over the Foundation's assets. That's not what I had in mind. I wanted a merger wherein the fundamental autonomy of the two organisations remained but the merger made mutual support and assistance possible. In my view we needed such a merger in the first instance to improve financial aid to students.

The governing Board (slowly) bought into the idea and made the merger happen—the idea of the College managing fundraising and the Foundation managing (with the College's assistance) their increasing assets. Alan Smith headed up the search that brought Randi Duke to the College. Initially some college departments weren't particularly happy because they themselves were engaging in fundraising and they were reluctant (at first) to join the larger project.

We needed a five-star board for the Foundation and Randi got very senior people in the private sector interested. Before Randi arrived, all I knew about fundraising were two principles: you've got to make friends before you can make money; and, it's the president who has to make "the ask" and get the gift.

So Randi and I were a team asking "big names" to join the Foundation board; we were remarkably successful at this.

Time for another story. One of the people we wanted on the Foundation board was Jim Pattison's right hand man. He and I spoke on the phone and I asked him to come to the College where we would share a sandwich in my office and then take a tour of the campus—all because, I told him, at the end I was going to ask him to join the Foundation board. At the time he was very busy with Pattison developments in China and I think with the coal terminal. He said he really couldn't undertake that commitment.

I said, well, come for the sandwich and the tour; he said he would, and he did. After the sandwich and chatting about the College and his obligations, we did the tour, and as I always did, if I bumped into one of our facilities crew, I'd stop and introduce him / her by name to my guest. I did that with faculty and staff we met in the hallways. I had major stopping points: the writing assistance program and the SARAW project were two of the stops.

When it was over, I thanked him for his time and said that whenever he felt a bit freer I would welcome his phone call to say that he was ready to join the Board. It was not that much later, may be two or three months later, I attended a meeting of the Foundation board (I was the corporate secretary of the Board) and there he was, a member of the Board.

He stayed for a year, as I recall; I often wondered how and why he had found the time to join the Board. It was not until much later that I learned from other sources that he had explained to the Board that when I had taken him on the tour he had been impressed by the fact that I knew employees by their name, and not only knew what their job was but had some personal story to share about each person to whom I introduced him. His explanation was that in the face of that performance he had to find a way to give a year of his time to the College and its Foundation.

Donations of various kinds began flowing in and we embarked on our first capital campaign, furnishing the Sportsplex.

6 Another core strategy had to do with facilities. After I was named president I learned that we were not on the list of colleges with whom the Ministry would discuss funding for capital facilities. Clearly that had to change. What's the first critical success factor here? Get Capilano College on the list of colleges with whom the Ministry will discuss capital facilities.

This prompts an aside.

6.1 A critical success factor is neither a procedure nor an action plan; it is simply a result. Those who are assigned the responsibility to achieve that result are free to formulate their own action plans, about which the only limitation is a set of actions or behaviours that are prohibited. In this case, an obvious prohibition would be that no bribery whatsoever of Ministry officials or others in government is acceptable.

Obvious, but I find it amazing just how many times I read of exactly such behaviour occurring in both the private and public sectors.

Alan Smith and Marie Jessup led the charge on this; the VPs and I made cooing noises from the sideline. Eventually we were not only on the list, but we were talking. There followed the Sportsplex, the classroom addition to the Library building, and finally Phase III with the performing arts theatre. All of these benefitted from the Resource Development office that we had established earlier.

I think the first Sechelt campus was another beneficiary of these times, or perhaps that was from an earlier incarnation of me in the CEO's office, or was it the Squamish campus. No, I think this has to do with the Sechelt campus because the first part of the story I'm going to tell happened in Pebbles, the restaurant that is part of the Driftwood Inn on the Sechelt waterfront, and the second part involves me and the governing Board.

ADM Jack Newberry and I had made a trip to Sechelt to view the existing rented facility occupied by the College, and to discuss funding for a permanent facility. We had lunch at Pebbles and got to talking about total square feet and the $ / square foot cost, and programs and services I wanted for the facility. I drew a bit of a floor plan on a napkin—no, that's the truth!—and we to'd and fro'd about various details. Eventually Jack said, we can do this. I looked him in the eyes and asked, Are we agreeing on the broad brush strokes of square footage, unit cost, funded programs and services for this facility? Yes, we are Doug. And we shook hands.

At the next meeting of our Board, I reported on the visit, the discussions and the agreement. The first question I got was, have you got all that in writing? I answered, No, that I had not asked for it in writing, nor had I written any "note to file." I was upset by this demonstrated lack of trust, but kept my cool and thought of a Charles Handy story. I doubted that any of them had ever heard of Charles Handy far less had read any of his work, so I told them Handy's story of "the Chinese contract."

His story is that he's a manager in South Malaysia for an oil company responsible, among other responsibilities, for negotiating agreements with Chinese dealers. At the conclusion of a negotiation, after drinking the ritual cups of tea and shaking hands, he took out the official company agreement form and began filling in the agreed upon numbers. The dealer said, if you think I'm going to sign that, you are mistaken. Handy said, but I'm only filling in the numbers we have just agreed on. The dealer replied, if we have agreed on them, why do you need a legal document. It makes me suspect that you have got more out of the agreement than I have, and intend to use the law to enforce your terms.

In my culture, the dealer said, a good agreement is self-enforcing because both parties go away seeing each other smiling. If either party does not smile, the contract is unenforceable, lawyers or no lawyers.

The lesson Handy drew from this experience is that compromise is a prerequisite of progress; about the need for trust and a belief in the future; the willingness to forego some present good to ward off future evil, i.e., spend now in order to gain later. To quote Handy: *The pursuit of our own short-term advantage, and the desire to win everything we can, will only perpetuate animosities, destroy alliances and partnerships, frustrate progress, and breed lawyers and the enforcement of bureaucracy.*

I taught his lesson and the Board agreed that they would wait for the universe to unfold, and that they hoped, to use a common phrase, that my ass would not end up in a sling at their hands. The story ends that without me ever putting anything in writing about our agreement at Pebbles, we got the new building under the terms of my agreement with Newberry, although Alan and the architects made a far better floor plan than I had laid out.

7 The last core strategy had to do with FTEs and funding and revenue streams and costs.

7.1 The critical success factors were not unlike those of facilities core strategy:

- we must get annual funding reductions to be smaller, or better yet, stop completely;
- we must get some additional funding on the margins for services, student support, and our community activities.
- we must get Cap's unit funding value raised from being the lowest (I think it was) to somewhere higher up in the ranking.

Frank, Greg and I were no slouches when it came to data analysis. This is not to exclude Marie. Her work was of a different kind because she looked at how we were spending our money and the value obtained for dollar spent while the old CoD team tended to look at performance, productivity and other types of ratios.

All four of us were at a disadvantage: we didn't have a complete set of province-wide data; all we had were bits and pieces of data subsets. This annoyed me and I pressed hard, probably bordering on belligerence, for a data dump. All to no avail; indeed it got to the point where my colleagues suggested I cool it. Years later, long after I had retired from Cap, I would hear that ADM Shell Harvey feared giving us the data because Jardine would ram "his" analysis of our (government) data down our throats.

Nope, it wasn't always pretty and tidy in the trenches.

7.2 Taken as a whole, this issue of obtaining sustainable funding for the College has to be seen as a slowly developing failure on my part—a failure in absolute terms, not a failure relative to how other colleges were doing, for government clawbacks and cutbacks were handed out to all. That I wasn't alone in this failure is faint comfort.

To counter this, my executive and I began discussing the matter of revenue stream development more frequently. I have a recollection that in a 1994 executive meeting I suggested that our non-government grant revenue plus our non-FTE-student fee revenue would have to increase significantly within the next two to three years. I vaguely remember putting a number on it and the reaction was along the lines of, what are you smoking, Doug?

I did not push a continuation of this discussion—another failure of courage? Was I already retired? Probably yes as far as the big issues that were just appearing on the edge of the radar screen were concerned. My crude idea (that I never shared with my executive) for attacking the revenue problem was to make Cap a joint government and private institution. Without attempting to recall my idea in any detail, just let me say that it was a nightmarish thought.

And then, in a moment it was all over, although the ending took several months to conclude. My first contract in 1986 was for five years. Pursuant to the fine print of my contract, the decision to renew my contract was made in 1990 for a term of three years (I didn't want to sign on for another five years) becoming effective in February 1991, to expire in February 1994. Again pursuant to the fine print, early in 1993 my contract was renewed again, for what I told the Board would be the last time. This renewal would take me through to 1996.

My habit was to go for a walk when I needed to be quiet and undisturbed for the purpose of thinking. On Thanksgiving weekend in 1993, I went for a long walk; the topic on my mind was how could I find the energy to fulfill my contractual obligation. I had suddenly found myself exhausted; instead of waking up bright eyed and bushy tailed, I found myself dreading another long day of work. Yes, I could tough it out, but that meant that I would increasingly be prone to making mistakes; no, that's not how I wanted this story to end. Better to tell the Board that I had to retire sooner rather than later, in fact within a year, than to stay on, make mistakes that would probably damage the College and leave my reputation in tatters. In short, I wanted out while I and the College were at the apogee of the curve.

I got home, informed my wife of what I had decided I must do, and then called Robin Wilson, the current chair. I need to see you, I said. Oh, what's up? How about next week, she asked. No, I said, I need to see you before I go back to the College after Thanksgiving. Can you tell me what it's about? No, I don't want to; I just want to see you and tell it to you face to face.

It was either the Sunday or the Monday of that holiday weekend that she received me in her home. I laid out my story; she accepted my verbal resignation to be effective at the Board's discretion but as soon as possible. She asked that I make no mention of this to anyone so that she had time for private discussions with Board members before anything was made public. That was no issue for me.

I returned home with a great sense of relief: I could make it through '94, but I knew I couldn't make it to '96.

Greg Lee was named president in the late fall of 1994, and took over the office in February 1995. When in 1994 it was made public that I would be retiring, I had one-on-one conversations with each member of my executive asking them if, regardless of an internal or external person being named president, did they think they would stay or leave. They all said they thought they would stay.

Events represent disjunctions in the curve of life; indeed, the curve of life is usually never a smooth extrapolation from yesterday or yesteryear to tomorrow or next year. Frank left to head up the BCCAT; Robert left to be a president elsewhere, eventually at Sheridan College; Geoff left to represent the BCMA (IIRC); Randi left due to a physical condition that made her unable to work; Marie left by mutual agreement. I would be surprised if Greg didn't feel naked: in a very short space of time the senior brain

> trust of the College for almost twenty years was no longer there—an extraordinary loss of corporate wisdom and memory.

I'm now at the end of this memoir, so this is the place to say that the Board chairs whom I served, all, without exception, had their own way of caring for me as president or acting principal. Robin's attention at that sudden meeting in her home, and her careful monitoring of me in the weeks thereafter until she was sure I was OK, were great acts of kindness.

I think of the one who at the end of our weekly (or was it biweekly) breakfast meeting, said, Doug, you seem particularly stressed out; let's go for a walk where I got a gentle lecture on the importance of stopping to smell the roses. Or another, who when I showed up at his / her home in advance of a public meeting and asked if I could catch a nap on the floor (I often slept on the floor in my own home, and still do—my back likes the firmness and I refer to it as sleeping on my tatami mat), showed me the plush carpeted living room and left me alone. Another Board chair, I am told, expressed to the Board the view "that this man deserves much more than we are paying him," and then made it happen.

That doesn't account for all the Board chairs I served, but it is the picture of all of them. And this is not to suggest that members of the Board did not also show their care for me at a personal level. It was, all told, a most satisfying experience.

MATH VIDEO PRODUCTION

TED BENTLEY

Math and video production are hardly a natural pairing, but in the early 1980s the Cap Math Department began experimenting with video tape production to supplement classroom instruction. At that time Capilano had a TV studio—officially called the Dynamics Lab—and following a mathematics conference at Lane Community College in Eugene, Oregon faculty members Bob Verner and I made a pitch to use the Lab during PD time to produce some instructional math tapes. Along with Bob and me, a number of Capilano math faculty (Bob Rennie, Alf Waterman, Wendy Lynn, Ken Towson, Frank Harris, Reimar Hauschildt) were ready to test their instructional skills in front of a TV camera.

We knew at the outset that we didn't want to just film one of us standing in lecture mode marvelling at the mysteries of math while writing out the details on a blackboard with our back turned to the viewer—rather, we wanted a more user friendly (or so we thought), one-on-one tutor format. Simple enough in concept but the Dynamics Lab had only huge studio cameras. No problem setting up a couple of cameras to film the instructor sitting down at a desk in tutor mode, but how to film the desktop that the instructor was to write on? No way could the superstructure of the Lab support a studio camera pointing down to the desktop.

So we creatively hung a large mirror from the superstructure on a 45-degree angle then aimed a camera at it, using reverse scan to correct the image. Nasty setup but we filmed a few early segments using the mirror until our colleagues on the media side (Peter Kellington and Cam Williams) noticed a periodic, somewhat nauseating sway in our desktop as we developed the ideas.

After much head-scratching (and dismissing the possibility that the instructor was the source of the nauseating element) our media colleagues discovered the source of the sway—the air conditioning system that came on periodically to bring down the intense heat generated by the studio lights. Technical complications aside, we considered the experiment a success, as did our students. They spoke positively about the early calculus and precalculus tapes and encouraged us to make more.

As the 80s marched on, we continued to experiment and produce tapes. We created the video masters in ¾ inch VHS tape and dubbed down the distribution copies to ½ inch VHS. Cameras shrank in size to the point that we could finally use a much smaller vertically mounted camera in addition to frontal cameras. Prior to filming, the instructor would write out the shell of the program content on 11 × 17 cardboard sheets that were then stacked on the instructor's desk ready to be filmed.

Typically we had one producer (Cam Williams) sitting in the Dynamics Lab control room, switching between the frontal and overhead cameras as one of us developed the mathematical concepts on the prepped sheets. No rehearsals and minimal advance scripting meant Cam and the instructor had to stay alert for camera changes between overhead and frontal shots. While post-production editing was technically possible (but tedious and costly for technician time on our non-existent budget), we basically filmed all the segments in one take. The pressure was on during production to nail the mathematics and not worry too much about our at times questionable media skills. Students continued to praise our efforts and used the tapes in the Math Lab, library and at home on their own VCRs.

The Apple IIe was released in 1983 and we discovered that it could be interfaced with a VCR, so our focus shifted to producing interactive videos. This involved filming a main instructional segment followed by a number of short remedial-type segments that served as attachments to the main program. We then laboriously tracked the video tape, marking possible entry points for the computer. As a student viewed a video, the instruction would pause at the predetermined track points with the computer posing a question on its monitor (separate from the video monitor). If the student answered correctly the video program would resume, but on an incorrect answer the instruction would branch to an attachment segment located elsewhere on the tape.

It was a nice idea but incredibly cumbersome to produce and painfully slow for the student to sit there waiting as the video tape mysteriously spun forwards and backwards to the various branch points. Effective, interactive computer-based learning was still a decade or so away.

While we abandoned interactive video development, we forged ahead into the early 90s, adding videos as a summer PD activity to our expanding collection of algebra, precalculus, calculus, probability and statistics tapes. The calculus series was sufficiently developed that we offered a self-paced version of Calculus I which used the videos as the primary source of instruction. ESL students also used the tapes extensively because they could stop, replay and focus on the English presentation of mathematical concepts that they might have already been exposed to but in a different language.

In 1991 a textbook representative from Worth Publishers, Bill Davis, happened to hear of our video exploits and said that he might be interested in contracting with us to produce tapes to accompany a new textbook on precalculus. Following discussions on publisher expectations married with producer realities, a contract was signed between me, Capilano College and Worth Publishers. In 1992 Worth published the Video Tutor series consisting of 150 tapes (120 hours of video) and accompanying workbook, The Video Tutor Guide. While not exactly best-sellers, they were well received by students studying math at Capilano and elsewhere in Canada and the US.

Although the tapes continued to be well used by students throughout the 90s, our production fell off. As VCRs became extinct we ported some of the Video Tutor tapes onto CDs in 2005—ironically the same year that YouTube uploaded its first video, introducing a new standard for video distribution.

While some of the tapes continue to be used by today's students at Capilano, our video exploits are now not much more than sidebar curiosities in the history of Capilano and the technological timeline of educational video production and distribution. However the videos formed an important component of life and learning in the Mathematics Department of the 80s and 90s for both faculty and students.

TWO TALES FROM ADULT BASIC EDUCATION

LIZ YOUNG

Robin Hood in ABE

I'M A SUCKER for challenges. Thirty-two years of Adult Basic Education provided them weekly. Perhaps the most endearing challenge was a Persian boy I'll call Mo. I had an overload in the biology class the day that Mo started the course. He sat at the back with the tattooed boy. At the front of the class, another new student muttered to himself through the introductory lecture and swatted imaginary flies.

I gave the lecture, set up the self-paced assignments, and got the new students working while I went into the lab to help the ongoing students. When I returned to the class, Jerry, one of my nursing students, informed me that there had been an incident in class.

"The class got noisy," he said. "The crazy guy at the front stood up and told the tough looking one at the back that he should be sent to a concentration camp."

"And . . . ?" I asked.

"The tough one stood up and told the crazy one that if he knew what was good for him, he'd sit down, and shut up . . . like NOW! He looked gob-smacked but he sat down and shut up."

I took the crazy one and set him up in the exam room. I took Mo out of class and explained that we try to accommodate all types and if another incident occurred to call me.

He nodded. "You know he's a nut case."

My turn to nod. "He still has a right to be here."

"I was helping. I'm good with nutters."

Weeks later, Mo waded into biology, accumulating a following of girls who were clearly into bad boys and wanted to form a study group. Mo looked and sounded like Di Niro in *Taxi*. He rolled up his T-shirt one morning to reveal a tattoo stretched from one shoulder to the other that declared "Fuck This World" in Algerian script. He wore a solid gold chain and carried a roll of dollar bills in his pocket. Because the new tattoo hurt, one of the girls left to buy Vaseline and the others watched enviously while she massaged it into Mo's back. He gave me his "This is the way to do it" smile.

The following week, Mo brought a notice that required him to go into the interior to answer a charge. A fight in a club resulted in a fatal stabbing and while Mo had not wielded the knife, he was charged as an accessory. I didn't want to lose him. His influence on some of the attention deficit students, particularly the pretty ones, had taught me the value of incentive.

I gave him a letter for his lawyer. I praised his enthusiasm and industry.

"It won't work," he said. "This is not my first charge. I might not see you for a year or so."

He returned two weeks later. He expressed surprise that a letter could have saved him. Clearly, he didn't put much faith in the written word.

"I got off with twenty hours of community service. I owe you," he said.

Later that day, I complained that my taped lectures needed to be updated. He offered to film them all and copy them for me. His probation officer called me later and confirmed that while he had some dangerous friends, he was safe to meet me at the College and cover field trips for me.

He brought "his mother's camera," an expensive beast, and a girl friend, who looked hot off the runway, although she chewed gum most of the time. Periodically she ran out of candy and he gave her more money to restock. "I like to keep my women satisfied," he said.

On the Lighthouse Park field trip, we took his harem and his girlfriend. He was good with the camera, capturing fawn lilies between the cracks of the rocky paths. At the rocky outcropping, I sat down to demonstrate the leaf difference in False Box and *Arctostaphylus uva ursi* and missed the stone. I started to roll down the sheer rock below me. I heard one of the girls say, "Look at Liz," then felt Mo's fist around my arm as he hauled me from the edge. I felt awkward and a bit embarrassed but when I looked down, I saw how close I was to the edge. The kid might have saved my life.

While we were filming, he told me that he and other Persian kids were bullied at school. "We got together," he said. "We bought T-shirts for the kids and put our logo on it. When they were bullied, we got together and met the bullies with baseball bats. After a while, we got calls from kids in other schools and went to protect them. Soon the bullying stopped. Nobody touched a kid in our T-shirts. That's how you deal with bullying."

"That's how you form gangs," I thought.

At the faculty / staff Christmas party, the Dean and the Divisional Assistant mentioned the telephone calls. A woman had called everyone in the department threatening death to anyone who spoiled "her boy's faith" with the influence of science. She read sections of an encyclopedia, or The Koran. She threatened to kill us all, and followed with a lecture on the evils of meat-eating. I remember Mo asking me if science would destroy his faith; his parents were worried. I said that it didn't have to change his beliefs.

Mo's mother was obviously very ill. I worried that he wouldn't come back in spring. The dean called him to let him know that we understood, but his mother answered the call.

"She threatened to hang me from a crane," he said.

Mo came back, and when I told him of the calls, he shrugged. "She can't help it. She's a paranoid schizophrenic. She threw my father out and I've looked after her since I was ten."

He completed his courses and did well although our morning messages totalled as many as forty-four garbled death threats at least once a week.

Years later, when I retired, a call from work passed Mo's father's number to me. I called and his father asked me if I would visit the correctional centre because Mo had graduated to major fraud and needed to occupy himself in jail.

I went to see a more muscular version of the boy. His head was shaved and he had lost a front tooth and acquired some scars on his face, but his smile and his spirit were still intact. He looked good in orange. He had made and lost millions. He knew all the Vancouver gangs but had not joined any of them. He knew most of the VPD and North Shore RCMP too. As far as he was concerned, he was a Robin Hood, although I doubt that he gave much to the poor. He'd been arrested in take-downs, in helicopter stings. He'd rescued girls in distress. He'd been a bodyguard and inherited a club from the man he protected, all before the age of twenty-four. He showed no inclination for repentance.

I took him on with a distance TRU course in literature. He did well. During his next sentence he decided on business courses and came out to get a business certificate at BCIT. He met a twenty-first century Cleopatra with brains and a very straight family. He runs a business now that somehow manages to stay on the right side of the law, or so he tells me. He drives a BMW and lives in a penthouse suite. He claims that it is a consequence of all the critical thinking he learned from Capilano!

I sometimes miss the kid with the crazy mother, who saved my life, and survived on his own generated charisma.

Excuses to Excellence: Nadya's story

One of her teachers said that she'd never finish high school. Her dyslexia had been demonstrated in all her tests. Still, she came to ABE, although she arrived late and left early. On her computer screen, the words formed according to the sounds without punctuation or structure as if she were getting it all out while she remembered what it was she wanted to say.

Already retired, I stood in for her English instructor in a crowded self-paced class, and each time Nadya left the class I despaired. My brief week with the class ended and I called Nadya to ask if she would like some one-to-one tutoring. I thought she would decline the offer but she turned up.

We started on spelling and punctuation, with numerous stops for tea, or conversation to punctuate her attention lapses. I didn't think I would see much of her in the following weeks but she surprised me. She was always late and still left early, but she worked on her spelling, learned some rules and their exceptions, and surprised me with nineteen out of twenty on her first test. More importantly, she surprised herself and wanted to progress to essay structure.

A week later she surprised her father, who also taught at Capilano, with a finished essay. With each success, her attention span grew and she started to turn up on time with new ideas. Six months later, she registered for first year courses and completed two with grades of B+. In the next semester she took a science and scored an A.

Nadya completed her Capilano two-year diploma and applied to both University of Victoria and UBC. She is now at UBC in third-year History of Fine Arts, earning A grades and high B's. One of her papers is deemed publishable. Her phonetic spelling has all but disappeared.

She doesn't need a tutor now but still turns up at my house to study and write her papers. She plans to do her Master of Arts degree in Architecture. In five years she has shaken off the labels that afflict a lot of entering ABE students and proved herself to be a confident academic.

Wherever I go now, I bump into former ABE students who have gone farther than they expected: the boy who wanted his grade twelve for auto-mechanics is now a dental surgeon; the girl who couldn't see any future for herself is now a radiographer; the young man who developed a taste for literature is now teaching and writing it; the First Nations student who was told to finish school is now the education advisor for the Squamish Band.

Nadya, whose tested results showed a limited future, should finish her degree in a year and looks forward to a career in architecture.

The Capilano Review, Spring 1972 / 1.1
Cover image: Jeff Keen, *Amazing Ray Day*
(COURTESY MICHAEL MORRIS, IMAGE BANK, THE WESTERN FRONT)

TOWARD A CAP COLLAGE

PIERRE COUPEY

When I think back on faculty creativity over the last few decades at Capilano, née College, now University, and how that volatile creativity turned Cap into a kind of Black Mountain College North for its first decades, it's hard to know where to start, and already we know it's impossible to cover all of it. Maybe this anthology will stitch something of a collage together, a first crack at a collective self-portrait.

Even to summarize one's own time there, let alone that of all the colleagues and events that made our lives so rich at Cap, is reductive, a matter of lists. For example:

Started teaching at Capilano College in 1970, 28 years old, retired from full time teaching in 2003, 61 years old & 10th most senior person in the institution, then taught part-time at the English department's request for another eight years until 2011. Retired completely at 69, now 71.

Spent the majority of my adult life, 41 years, working at Cap. In that time founded The Capilano Review, *the Humanities Division Poetry Reading Series, and the Koerner Lecture Series. At various times served on and chaired the Humanities Division evaluation committee, served as an English department coordinator and Humanities Division summer coordinator, served on Creative Writing Articulation Committees, served as Chief Steward of the CCFA, and served on numerous all-College committees, including two Capilano Foundation committees. Etc.*

None of that gives the juice of the place, the energy we all felt there, the charge of charging around, from class to class, from meeting to meeting, from crisis to crisis, from failure to success. For most of us at Cap from the early days—teaching there, being there—it wasn't just a job: it was a passion, a matter of love, an opportunity for growth, a further higher education, a profound and extensive conversation with dynamic students and colleagues.

So here are some fragments toward a Cap collage, starting with the key element, the ground as it were, for what we did there: teaching. And for me, teaching in the English department meant getting to work alongside faculty whose passion for teaching, for language and literature, for fiction and poetry and drama, inspired students in all their classes, inspired students to discover themselves and their potential.

Bill Schermbrucker lured me from UBC where I was finally finishing my MA in Creative Writing and English after a few years split between painting full time on a Canada Council grant and starting *The Georgia Straight*. The Department then consisted of a South African and American expats—Bill, Crawford Kilian, Jim Terral, Frances Burstein are the names I remember now—the only other Canadians being Jean Clifford, and David MacKinlay. Bill was our coordinator, one of the most influential persons in the life of Cap, and certainly in my life: judicious, calm, sensible, reasonable, ambitious and *visionary*.

Bill believed in full academic freedom, and as instructors we were free to pursue our strengths and create course outlines and reading lists that reflected who we were as individuals, so we could bring the best of ourselves to the students. Yes, there was something of a framework: rough number of assignments, office hours, grading profiles, class lists to keep, and classes to meet. Apart from that, complete freedom and openness to experimentation. And Bill fought the administration to preserve that freedom for us, even when some of our experiments were disasters, even when some of us in our blithe ignorance and disregard for authority and academic rules crossed lines we didn't even know were there.

And the students: yes, we despaired at how woefully unprepared most of them were for first-year university level work, for doing deep reading, writing essays, research papers, *and for participating in class discussion.* For that was the hallmark of the openness of our teaching approach at Cap: the classroom was a place for dialogue and debate between instructor and students, between students themselves. It was a forum for ideas, responses, passionate interpretations and arguments about what mattered in a story, a poem, a novel, a play: the classroom was a place *of continuing crisis, for the critical, for determining what mattered.* More often than not I'd leave a class completely exhausted. But happy and high, too.

We were not there "to blather" at students, as Dr. Bulcroft recently put it.

I think the students then could sense we were working things out, for ourselves and with them, from a position almost of *tabula rasa,* that we were not there to dully repeat dogmas or *idées reçues.* And they met us with their own enthusiasm, their own hunger to learn. We were there to discover, together. Of course, most of us came from rebellious contexts and situations wherein we defied authority and authorities, so we could hardly set ourselves up as such—in fact we encouraged them to defy us, and any and all arbitrary authority as well. I believe this spirit lives on at Cap, and believe this spirit is what defines us at our best.

For me, it was in the Creative Writing classes that the fullest openness of approach, discovery, debate and critique became possible: I loved those three-hour evening blocks when students distributed copies of their latest magnum opus, then read it out to the class, and then we all fell upon it like bees on a wild flower, or wolves on a wounded elk, and then worked the damn thing over until it emerged glistening like a polished bone, a stone rounded by surf, a flower tilted to the sun. OK, not to get too carried away with bad similes, but those CW classes were often extraordinary events, sometimes works of art in and of themselves, wherein we all discovered capacities we did not yet know. And all of it in recognition of how hard it was to make something that could become memorable.

And students produced memorable work. I will never forget Rojeanne Allworth's poems evoking the turquoise shimmer of swimming pools at midnight, or Jancis Andrews' shocking poem "The Blood Tie," and we published them both in *The Capilano Review.*

And then there were the classes of CW students who continued their creative writing meetings long after the terms ended, for years, and ended up marrying each other, divorcing, re-marrying, publishing, continuing their lives together. And then the tandem CW classes Bill and I taught simultaneously in Squamish because there was so much demand even in that small community, loggers and railway men and housewives and waitresses passionate about poems, about stories, about experience.

Several of these CW students became student editors on the editorial board of *The Capilano Review*—Steve Harris, who is now a distinguished professor of Art History at the University of Alberta; Wendy Pickell, who worked closely with Bill as the student fiction editor; and Janice Harris who eventually became a long-serving District of North Vancouver council member.

The Capilano Review, Capilano's literary and visual arts magazine, the magazine that Bill challenged me to start in 1971, became an integral part of the English department's vision of itself as a creative force: we all saw it as the nucleus of a dynamic agenda that interwove teaching, readings, and publishing. Our English department was then, as it is now, largely made up of instructors who practice the craft of writing as professionals, as poets and fiction writers—Bill, Gladys Hindmarch, Bob Sherrin, Sharon Thesen, Daphne Marlatt, Crystal Hurdle—plus those who, like Reid Gilbert, Graham Forst and Jenny Penberthy among others, did scholarly research and published books and critical articles in Canadian and American journals. And now Kim Minkus, Ryan Knighton, Roger Farr, Reg Johannson and other new faculty.

The Capilano Review, which celebrated its 40th anniversary in 2012, has been and continues to be in the vanguard of little magazines in Canada and abroad, and as such functions not only as the flagship of our English department and Humanities Division, but also as one of the flagships of Capilano University itself.

Throughout its history *TCR* has published, sometimes for the first time, an amazing number of Canada' most celebrated literary names. In 1974 my colleagues gave me a wonderful gift, a hardbound copy of the first five issues of *The Capilano Review*. Here's a short who's who of who we published in those first issues: Earle Birney, Phyllis Webb, John Newlove, George Bowering, Andreii Voznesensky, Evgenii Evtushenko, Bill Bissett, Dr. Brute, Gerry Gilbert, Susan Musgrave, Patrick Lane, Tom Wayman, Nicanor Parra, Jack Hodgins, Lionel Kearns, John Pass, David Phillips, bpNichol, Brian Fisher, D'Arcy Henderson, Gladys Hindmarch,

Christos Dikeakos, Audrey Thomas, Victor Coleman, Warren Tallman, Stan Persky, and more, including many CW students from Cap.

When I showed the first issue of *TCR* with its b/w *Amazing Ray Day* cover by Jeff Kean to Tony Emery, who was then the Acting Director of the Vancouver Art Gallery, he whistled: *Are you trying to get fired?* Then as now, *TCR* was prepared to publish work that was distinctly experimental, non-academic and subversive. We were prepared to push the edges, because that was also our teaching mandate.

And so much of that is the result of the hard work over the last four decades of a succession of stellar editors: Bill Schermbrucker, Ann Rosenberg, Dorothy Jantzen, Bob Sherrin, Sharon Thesen, Ryan Knighton, Brook Houglum and Jenny Penberthy, and the contributions of so many faculty and students who served as associate editors, editorial assistants, and on various editorial boards: Crawford Kilian, Jean Clifford, Pat Hutchinson, Reid Gilbert, Jim Terral, Katherine Alliston, Paul Crombie, Daphne Marlatt, Penelope Connell, among others, impossible to list them all. And though the days of the editorial board and its marathon editorial meetings and debates are long gone, much of the spirit of those days survives among those of us who serve on the The Capilano Press Society Board: Colin Browne, George Stanley, Andrew Klobucar, Roger Farr, Crystal Hurdle, Elizabeth Rains, to name a few of the usual suspects.

The collective creativity of these faculty made *TCR* a magnet for Cap, and through its dynamic we were able to start and sustain two adjuncts to the magazine—the Humanities Division Reading Series and the Leon and Thea Koerner Lecture Series—and attract writers from across Canada (and the States) to come to Cap to give public readings, talks and visit CW classes. A later spin-off has been the very successful *TCR* and Humanities Division sponsored Writer-in-Residence Program.

As I recall, the first reading held at Cap was organized by Reid Gilbert when he invited Phyllis Webb, and in 1974 we launched the Canada Council funded Humanities Division Reading Series and over the years hosted a succession of major and emerging writers, including Robin Blaser, Margaret Atwood, Michael Ondaatje, George Bowering, Victor Coleman, bpNichol, John Newlove, DG Jones, Sheila Watson, Duncan McNaughton, August Kleinzahler, Brian Fawcett, Roy Kiyooka, Michael Turner, George Stanley, Barry McKinnon, to name only a very few. In the early years the reading series was very intense, with four readings in the fall and four in the spring.

And once we had the writers here, we more often than not both tape-recorded and videotaped their readings and talks, and interviewed them for *TCR*. Jenny Penberthy, as a recent editor of *TCR*, and as founder of our website, has done heroic work in regathering these archival materials and making much of it available on-line on the *TCR* website. For most of these documents we have Cam Williams to thank, who was then in the Audio-Visual Department at Cap, for providing the technical assistance and means.

Many of these readings became memorable occasions in and of themselves, especially the Ondaatje, Atwood, Watson and Blaser readings. All the readings gathered large audiences from across Vancouver, and Cap, along with The Western Front, was one of the exciting places to be to hear the latest and the best. The overflow crowd for the Atwood reading alone meant that we had to improvise closed-circuit TV coverage in adjacent classrooms at the last minute. Students at Cap at the time were so energized by all these events that they often comprised the largest cohort at readings elsewhere in the city, particularly at The Western Front.

Our distinctive Creative Writing classes, *The Capilano Review*, the Reading Series and the Koerner Lectures, and now the Writer-in-Residence Program and the advent of CUE Books (Capilano University Editions), have all grown from and contributed to the dynamic creativity of the faculty and students in the English department at Capilano, and it is this culture of faculty inspired projects that has made CapU the singular institution it has become and can continue to be, but only if the faculty *continue to be served* by the administration—by deans, vice-presidents, presidents—who understand that their role in the equation is to be supportive of faculty innovation and of faculty participation in the governance of the institution.

For it has to be said that none of what we did could have happened if our coordinators and colleagues, our departments and divisions, our deans and vice presidents and presidents, had not been fully and deeply supportive of what we as faculty dreamed up and dreamed of achieving. In particular I want to thank the following Administrators for their understanding and support for *TCR* over the years: Robert Campbell, Penny LeCouteur, Dorothy Jantzen, Carol McCandless, Frank Gelin, Bill Gibson, Greg Lee, Doug Jardine, Paul Gallagher, Harold Kirchner, and Leslie Brooks.

A tradition of excellence and creativity was fostered by all of them, and even though we may have fought one another tooth and nail in other arenas, when it came to the culture of Cap they knew the faculty could be, and had to be, trusted to generate the goods, as they are the direct interface with what counts most—the students.

The Capilano Review, Fall 2011 / 3.15
Cover image: Robert Keziere, Geoffrey Smedley's
Machine Room, Gambier Island
(COURTESY ROBERT KEZIERE)

RETAIL FASHION / MERCHANDIZING AT CAPILANO COLLEGE, 1972–1995

HILARY CLARK

HAROLD KIRCHNER, Career Dean, in 1972 asked me to research and to initiate a Retail Fashion / Merchandizing Program for inclusion in the career offerings already in place in the new Capilano College. To this end I was sent to San Francisco and Los Angeles to investigate the very successful Fashion Institute of Design and Merchandizing. I used its template to create a two-year program that included trade components, college basics such as English, and practical field work.

There was as yet no department, so I also went on a speaking tour of the Lower Mainland high schools to encourage students to enroll in the new program. This involved speaking in school classes as far away as Pemberton, and as close as Sutherland. My success was evident in a first-year enrollment of 38 students who met in the pottery lab (!) of after-hours West Vancouver High School.

In that there were no courses and no faculty, I also had the pleasure of putting together a two-year program of course outlines, finding and ordering text books and hiring faculty. From the outset the department was very democratically run, since none of us had a firm idea of what we were creating, and we needed complete collegiality to design an all-inclusive body of courses for our students.

The program moved around in the years before a campus was designed and built. We taught in Sunday school rooms, several high schools and in a warehouse on Welch Street in North

Vancouver. The last one we shared with the art department and had the unique pleasure (?) of running into nude models on platforms on our way to coffee. We shared faculty office space next to the only washroom, and it had a habit of providing excitement with a regularly overflowing toilet!

Eventually the campus was provided with portable classrooms, and a few faculty offices. We shared ours with Outdoor Recreation and Communications. As we were approaching the funding for a new building for the Career Programs I was asked to design a classroom that would be tailored specifically to the needs of the retailing students.

At that time we were still offering fashion design, so needed tables for drafting and sewing. As we modelled our garments in a yearly fashion show we required a modelling ramp, and mirrors. We studied fabrics and required sinks, Bunsen burners and a washer / drier. Lockers and a change room were on the list, and an area for selling items in our own store, The Campus Cupboard.

I insisted on a fitness program that was accommodated in the new field house with Joe Iacobellis. (He managed to court and to marry one of my best students!) We also used the track and showers on a regular basis. This was based on the belief that if one was going to sell clothes and other fashion items, one had to look the part, and being fit contributed to that.

Once we were housed in our specifically designed studio, the program grew to two first-year classes and one second-year class. The attrition was a success story in part as first year students accepted jobs leading from their practicums and didn't return for second year.

Even though we had the ramp and the mirrors in the studio, the audiences for our fashion shows grew to the point that we began renting North Vancouver's Centennial Theatre for our shows. We had stopped offering fashion design during this period because we didn't want to conflict with Kwantlen College, which was presenting an excellent design program. But since fashion shows were an integral part of fashion merchandizing, we continued by using clothing from local stores. The students learned to create the entire production. They planned the theme, found the clothes, made the sets, arranged the music and commentary and modelled the garments. No one was allowed to back out. One year we had three pregnant students model maternity clothes! We also involved the children of the students and faculty.

The highlight for me was the year we presented "CAP-tivation!", a name thought up by our fabric arts teacher, Eleanor Best. I actually wrote the script for that one as a musical set in Paris which used two students from the music program as the singing protagonists and a pit orchestra made up of students, faculty and friends. Recognizing that our students weren't actors, the leads mimed dialogue that was spoken "voice-over" from the sound room. Karin Plato, the female lead, is still making waves in Canada as a jazz singer. The students not only modelled, but also sang some choruses. That evoked some anxiety!

On the request of our president, Doug Jardine, who told me that CAP-tivation was the best thing he had seen produced to that date by the College, we went on to present a shorter re-write that same summer, at Expo 86. The Expo theme was transportation. A close friend of mine, Char Bowman, had taught a course for Community Education in small aircraft construction. He designed and constructed the sets and lighting for the Centennial Theatre production in the spring, and in the fall, he created a show around the idea of flying cars of the future. Again a pit orchestra was used to accompany the models. My son, Andrew Clark, a UBC music student at the time, conducted a 25-piece band and I got to play the piano.

Built into the program were weekly practicums set up in retail establishments. The students were marked on their work experiences. There were also many field trips ranging from a week at the Fashion Mart, to a midterm trip to the West Edmonton Mall where talks were arranged with the various retailers. The favourite trips were to San Francisco / Los Angeles to study the fashion industry, alternating yearly with either Montreal or Toronto. Lectures were set up ahead of time with the various stores / factories / studios, and students wrote detailed reports on what they had learned. The income from the fashion shows was used to subsidize the students' costs for these trips.

As budget cuts began to raise their ugly heads, the department was under siege as other programs wanted our sections. We were one small group, with only one full-time faculty member, me, who was also shop steward, against many other areas who felt their needs were more important than the Retail program's.

We spanned an interesting area of study in that we covered both art and business. Beginning in the Arts building, we were eventually moved over to the business area in the H building. There I had to redesign an existing space to accommodate the needs of our program. It was never as successful as the space in the original building, but brought the students nearer to the business courses and faculty.

We had an excellent record for student placement and success in the market place, and a hard-working faculty to ensure this continuity in the future. We even had students with degrees apply to gain market place expertise.

The stress of fighting for my department eventually affected my health, and I was invalided out in 1990. I knew that when I left, the department would be cannibalized for sections. It was, and is now a one-year certificate program.

The original concept of a retail fashion / merchandizing program that required skills training, theory and academic courses was a good one. As I said repeatedly to the administration, "We educate as well as train." This was evident in the course titles: Merchandizing, Marketing, Computer Skills, Sales Promotion, A Social Survey of Western Civilization, Business Communications, Career Readiness, Interior Design, Fabric Studies, Public Speaking.

The downturn in the economy affected the funding, I know, but by the end of my time we had articulated and achieved transfer accreditation with the Fashion Institute of Design and Merchandizing in California and at Ryerson in Toronto. Our students could go on if they wished to complete a degree at either institution.

The retired faculty continue to be delighted by the success in the marketplace of twenty years of exceptional students taught by a very dedicated group of faculty members.

PRIMED, TUNED UP, AND READY TO WORK: THE AUTO JOB ENTRY PROGRAM AT CAPILANO COLLEGE

MARTY WITTMAN

IT WAS THE MID-80S and the Canadian economy was taking most of us on a rollercoaster ride. We had just peaked a nationally unprecedented inflationary period and endured a failed federal policy of wage and price controls, followed by wild swings in the consumer price index. We also saw unemployment rates, especially among 18–24-year-olds, climb into the high teens. In many aspects, it was the worst of times, and Capilano College was not immune to the impact of those events.

The political winds blowing through Victoria played havoc with everyone's daily lives. Education was no exception: K-12 and post-secondary funding were particularly hard hit in our province. Fittingly, in 1985, Crawford Kilian released his book *School Wars* in which he decried and documented the devastation throughout the province.

So what was to be done at our beloved Cap to stave off the prospect of 5, 10, and 15 % proposed cutbacks? As a full-time instructor in the Communications Department, a department that was constantly on the verge of shrinking into oblivion, I responded to this dilemma in the usual fashion: Go do something about it!

Whereas some years previous, Bill Vander Zalm, as the Socred Minister of Human Resources, had proposed to deal with the "welfare crisis" in BC by handing out shovels, I proposed to hand out wrenches at Cap College—mechanics' wrenches. And thus came the launch of one of the most unlikely programs ever to be offered at Cap: the Auto Job Entry Program.

With cutbacks, real and perceived, swirling about on campus, I focused on putting together a proposal for the newly implemented Canadian Jobs Strategy Program commonly known as CJS. This was, of course, done off the side of my desk, so to speak, with the permission—and possibly even blessing—of our president, dean, and treasurer. Equally important was the co-operation of the Continuing Education Department in providing the umbrella administration under the leadership of Louise Krohn.

The intent of the proposal was simple enough: to create a win-win-win situation whereby Cap College would provide the facilities, staffing, and administration to train 100 students (age 18–24), all being in receipt of either income assistance or unemployment insurance. An integral part of this six-month program was to place these students with "Host Employers" who would participate as on-the-job trainers and eventually assist in providing the transition to employment in the automotive aftermarket service sector.

My previous business experience in setting up retail service centres in the automotive field throughout the Lower Mainland would prove to be quite an asset in that I had established a considerable network with dealerships, auto body, and general repair shops. Within a few weeks, I had assembled a pile of "Letter(s) of Intent" from some 60 host employers. This formed one of the many appendices to complement the proposal.

Once the proposal was submitted, the decision to fund the program came very quickly; it only needed the final approval of the local Member of Parliament, and that support was in place—due, no doubt, to the good efforts of our President Douglas Jardine.

There were, however, a few changes and provisos: Our proposal had been deemed to be somewhat too ambitious, and as a result, the funding was for 60 trainees (three intakes of 20). Also, the program was to be designated as a "Pilot Project". This was very common with CJS programs in that it committed federal funding for "one-time" only unless the project achieved a number of objectives.

All Job Entry programs funded by CJS were assigned to a project officer for supervision and review, and it was Robert Rae who filled that role in the first few years. We quickly and easily developed a working relationship. As a civil servant who had been a philosophy student, a former VW Canada employee, and an enthusiastic restorer of classic sports cars, Robert was equally at ease discussing the labour demands of the automotive aftermarket service industry and the divergent interpretations of Kirkegaard's writings.

With the green light to proceed, I was able to start making more solid plans and commitments, always under the watchful eyes of Greg Lee and Marie Jessup, of course. In taking up the role as coordinator of the Auto Job Entry Program, I freed up a number of sections in Communications that could be assigned to others in the department and I got on with the task of preparing to launch the program in the fall semester of '86.

A major component of the program required us to put together a concise curriculum, but we first needed to find an automotive instructor. Tom Mills, after much persuasion and verification that we had been approved for the project, left his high school teaching position in Mission to become the anchor for the technical part of the program by creating the "Specific Occupational Skills" modules. His extensive automotive skills covered the range of mechanical repairs and auto body collision repairs.

Another part of the curriculum was called "General Occupational Skills" and it was composed of several modules. Among them was First Aid and CPR training, which was provided by Anna from the Outdoor Recreation Department. Another module was Orientation to Safety in the Workplace, courtesy of personnel provided by WCB. In particular, Hardy Goetsch, the Safety Officer assigned to our program, proved to be most effective and flexible in accommodating our students, many of whom had ESL challenges. Over the 6–7 year span of the Auto Job Entry Program, we never had a serious injury either off- or on-site. This may well have been due to some of the footage of horrid and gory industry accidents that he made all students watch!

Yet another component of all CJS programs was "Life Skills," and it was Val Hunter, part-time instructor at SFU, who took up the challenge to deliver this essential and required component to students who were most reluctant to acknowledge their need of such instruction / guidance. (Remember, they had all registered for one sole reason: to work on cars.) On many occasions, Val became a "life saver" by negotiating with a student's parole officer to allow for continuation in the program instead of incarceration in the Valley. (Yes, many of these students came with a storied past.)

Finally, to round out the classroom curriculum, a number of instructors from the Adult Basic Education Department provided numeracy and literacy skills upgrading. Bob Irvine taught the Introduction to Computer Skills, and, in those early days of computer usage, Bob created some innovative databases for the program. In particular, I remember the list of several hundred host employers / automotive businesses, complete with contact information, and a tracking system for 1- ,3- and 6-month follow-ups with our graduates. The latter was yet another requirement of all CJS programs—well before Victoria required anything similar for public post-secondary institutions in BC.

The objectives of the program, as referenced earlier, were as follows: intake had to include a certain percentage of visible minorities, aboriginals, people with disabilities, and women in non-traditional trades. It was this last category that proved to be the most challenging. (Years later, this barrier gave birth across Canada to new Job Re-Entry programs under such names as "Women in Trades" and "Women in Trades and Technology".)

Another aspect of the "Pilot Project" designation (and program objective) spoke to the all-important 80% completion rate and 80% employment rate within three months. Given the total commitment of all the instructors and support staff, as well as the host of "Host Employers" throughout those years, we easily met and exceeded those objectives. As such, the program funding was renewed six times.

Indeed, while initially delivering the Auto Job Entry Program in a number of portable and "P" Building classrooms (remember the cutbacks and empty spaces), we had to move the program off-campus because it had outlived hard times; by the late 80s, the classrooms on Lynnmour campus were once again filling up with students in the more traditional Cap programs.

And so, I will put the "brakes" on describing the many adventures of those memorable and heady years. I could tell you about the first "tech facility" that Tom Mills created in one of the parking lots. (Later we leased spaces in auto repair centres and eventually even a few bays at VCC.)

I could also tell you about my embarrassment at being summoned to the Dean's office because a few of our students, on more than one occasion, had whistled at female students enrolled in the Secretarial and Legal Assistant programs.

And finally, if space and attention-span permitted, I could tell you about the graduates of that program who went on to complete their apprenticeship in mechanics or auto body, and have enjoyed careers, indeed thrived, in those fields as service managers and owners of their own automotive aftermarket service centres.

As a footnote to the CJS programs and Capilano College, I am pleased to point out that Capilano was funded for several other projects / programs after the start of the Auto Job Entry Program. In particular, I was humbled by the acceptance of the proposal in the following year to launch the "Personal Care Attendant for the Disabled" program (PCAD) in the Health Department which provided much-needed trainees / workers in this field. Also, I was pleased to see Jolene Bordewick get CJS funding to work with many disadvantaged youth in later years at Capilano College. Finally, my apologies for the many omissions of people and names, all of whom made these programs come to life and fruition.

BUILDING THE BUSINESS PROGRAM

CHARLES PRIESTER

IT STARTED WITH a job interview with Dean Harold Kirchner as a result of an ad in the *Vancouver Sun*, seeking faculty to help build a "business program" for Cap College.

The key point I made at the interview was that "We have to create a program that will attract students in spite of the fact we are an unknown quantity; don't have UBC's reputation; and have to prove ourselves. To succeed we need a different product." I think this statement got me the job to set up the Business Program

Previously the career programs did offer a smattering of business courses—Accounting 1 & 2, Business Math, and Business Communication.

Unlike the Commerce programs at the big universities, I looked for potential faculty that had "practiced what they preached," that is, earned a living doing what they were going to teach.

I tried to create course outlines that reflected actual business practices that were used in small to medium enterprises. I was helped by the fact that I had a 17-year career as a banker focusing on small to medium enterprise finance.

I was lucky to find some damn good co-workers who shared this point of view. I felt strongly that students were to be evaluated "under pressure"; at least 60% of the marks from at least 2 closed-book in-class exams, 30% from assignments and 10% from papers. Other departments at the College disagreed with that, but Harold Kirchner backed me up.

Cap's Business Program was very much helped (especially in its early days) by our ability to hire part-time faculty from BCIT's School of Business—a hard-nosed, no-nonsense school—that made very heavy demands on its students as well as its faculty.

The reason Cap's Business Program was so successful was the amazing "job finding" record of our two-year grads. If my memory serves me correctly, fewer than 25% of our grads went on to further study. The majority got paying jobs upon leaving Cap. This surprised me, as I had assumed that well-heeled North Shore students would surely go on to the universities. But it turned out most of "our" students came from more humble North Vancouver backgrounds.

We would often invite owner / managers of medium-size companies as guest speakers to talk about the "reality of the workplace," something I was a great believer in. It turned out that those guest speakers often hired our grads later on.

I vividly remember a few UBC Commerce "refugees" who switched to us after the first term (or first year), fed up with 300-student classes, profs who did not know them, etc.

I made sure to "parade" these guys in front of our students to show them how much more fun AND better our Business Program was.

Finally, we received kudos from UBC and SFU profs who were impressed with the caliber of our students who chose to further their studies.

Cap was also known for its creative faculty, who were constantly introducing new topics and whole new programs. Eventually the Business Program divided into specialties—Accounting and Finance, Marketing, and Computer Studies.

In addition, whole new programs were introduced that were relevant and took the College to a higher level. An example is the post-baccalaureate Asia Pacific Management Program and eventually the addition of the Latin America Management Program. These programs were collaborative efforts by Career and Academic faculty and were exceptionally successful.

FROM LEGAL ASSISTANT STUDENT TO VICE PRESIDENT

VAL COCHRAN

My first introduction to Capilano College was as a student. A new part-time Legal Assistant Program was about to begin. I was doing this type of work in a law firm, but wanted to get certified for more recognition.

I showed up at the College from work on a sunny May day. I was in a suit and high-heeled shoes and had an appointment with a counsellor—Bob Bagshaw. Imagine my surprise when (about 35 minutes late), the counsellor walked out wearing a wrinkly t-shirt, baggy shorts and Birkenstocks! I wondered what kind of place this was.

It turned out he had no information on the program as it was brand-new and had just got funding that month. After I explained to him (in no uncertain terms) how disappointed I was in this process, he called the co-coordinator of the program, Wanda Tilley, who saw me immediately.

The first class was beginning in a week and I was enrolled in Litigation Procedures—a subject I was completely familiar with, but part of the program, so I figured I should just take it and get an A. After the course was over, I went to see Ms. Tilley again to tell her how completely I had just wasted my time: the instructor (a lawyer) knew very little about the procedures (I am sure a lot about the theory), I had to keep correcting him, and I could have done a much better job at teaching this course than he had.

Wanda said "You're hired," and I started teaching that one course in the fall term while working full-time at the law firm.

The Dean, Harold Kirchner, met with me (administrators met with new hires as a routine matter in those days). I remember the application form I had to fill in, and under "Marital status" I had put "happy." It was typical of Harold to say not that I was married, just that my marital status was a happy one.

After about three weeks into the term, Wanda managed to get two more sections and I found myself teaching another course, and eventually teaching in the now fully designed Legal Assistant Program.

That was one of the interesting things about the College in the early days. There was temporary funding available for programs to start up—so long as you could find the students to fill them. Wanda had a particularly creative mind and was busily creating all types of programs that got this temporary funding.

I remember in the early days that if you met a well-dressed individual on campus, that would be a Business faculty member or student! All the rest were very '70s in their style (t-shirts, blue jeans, etc.). We use to say anyone too radical for SFU came to Cap! It made for a very interesting grouping.

Once I started teaching full-time, I became involved in the Capilano College Faculty Association, first as a member, then secretary on the board, then vice-president and then president (twice), as well as a member of several bargaining teams. I was also on the board of the provincial organization (now called FPSE) as secretary and treasurer.

One memorable bargaining session saw the union about to go on strike the next morning at 6:00 a.m. Doug Jardine was the chief spokesperson for the College and the sticking point was long-term temporary employees getting regular appointments. Each bargaining year we managed to get a couple of extra regularizations in. This year we wanted quite a bit more—we started off with everyone who had worked half-time to full-time for 10 or more years. At the time I was non-regular faculty and had worked full-time for 13 years!

The College started with a few, we came back with much more, until it was make-or-break time for the strike to be called off.

My legal background came in handy when I decided to go for clarity and said to the College team, "We need 13—take it or leave it. And to be clear, I am number 11, Pat Hodgson (also on the union team) is 12 and we can't look too self-serving so we need the one more." That managed to do it!

I eventually went to law school and got my LLB. The College continued to offer me sections and I continued to teach through my articles and my labour law practice. Then I decided to return to the College full-time.

What made me continue to work at the College, and to take the bold step of becoming VP of Human Resources (while still president of the union), had very much to do with my colleagues. There was a lot of camaraderie, but more than that, we could be very proud of our institution. Faculty were very dynamic and created many unique programs, supported by the administration with respect to finding funding. We all worked as a team. There was no real distinction between Career and Academic faculty, so there was a lot of "cross fertilization" of courses and programming.

We were all proud when UBC gave advanced standing to Capilano Science students; the Art programs were second to none. We all celebrated the successes of the others. But many of the unique programs that gave the College a stellar reputation were from the Career side. That is not to say that our Academic faculty were not creative, it was just more difficult to get funding for unique programs in that area. However, the quality of the teaching drew students from far and wide—and deservedly so.

I retired after 35 years at the College, and enjoyed every moment of my teaching and administrative years.

STEPPING OUTSIDE OF THE CLASSROOM: AN ACADEMIC GOES POLITICAL

BILL SCHERMBRUCKER

Karen Ewing is a short woman whose stature makes her quite unthreatening—that and her soft voice, tinged with a slight mid-western American accent. So when she comes into my office at Capilano College with a smile, it seems to be just a pleasant visit from a colleague I seldom see, except at union meetings. Karen is a geographer in the Social Sciences division. Perhaps she was visiting someone else in Humanities, I think, and noticing me through the open door of *The Capilano Review* office, stopped for a friendly chat. Does my memory invent it, or did she actually begin her pitch by saying, "By the way. . . "? In any case, I was entirely off-guard as she propositioned me with a plan that would swamp my life for the next six months.

"You know the union won the Cogswell grievance?" she said. "But then we disagreed with the College about how the arbitrator's award should be implemented, and we had to go back to arbitration, which cost us another $45,000 in legal fees."

"Okay," I said, beginning to suspect that she was leading up to something

"So we were wondering—you had an educational leave, didn't you?"

"Yes. I had the first one awarded by the College. That was several years ago, 1975–6. I produced two textbooks out of it. One I wrote, and the other is an anthology I put together."

"Great! Well, we were wondering . . . you see in the latest collective agreement negotiations, the College has really dug in on educational leave, and it's going to have to go to arbitration. But after the Cogswell expenses, the union just can't afford more legal fees. We were wondering if you would take it on?"

Talk about something coming out of left field! Me act as the Faculty Association union's lawyer and present legal arguments in a hearing before an arbitrator?

"Karen, I'm not a lawyer. I don't have any experience that would qualify me to conduct an arbitration, let alone win it! Who would I be up against, some big Howe Street lawyers with mansions in West Vancouver or Shaughnessey?"

"It doesn't matter who you'll be up against. The arbitrator will be Bruce McColl. He's smart and tough and fair, and so are you, Bill. He acts for unions as well as employers. And as for training, our union lawyer, Leo McGrady, is teaching an intensive course next month in Arbitration Law. The union will pay for you to take it."

I have often wondered whether Karen had actually researched my background. Did she know that I had taken some law courses in my bachelor degree studies, on the way towards becoming a lawyer? Had she found out that my father was the senior partner in Nairobi's most prestigious law firm and President of the Law Society of Kenya? She could not have known that my grandfather was a magistrate, that my great-grandfather was the son of a Bavarian judge. Was it simply an accident that the union executive picked me to work this arbitration for them?

Actually, I knew more about arbitration than I had let on: in choosing the contents for my anthology textbook, I had searched for writing that exemplifies the "Scientific" aim in James L. Kinneavy's A *Theory of Discourse*. The "Scientific" aim has nothing to do with laboratories necessarily, but is defined as "to state a thesis and prove it by careful, valid logic." A perhaps surprising example I give in my textbook is, "A Literature or Fine Arts assignment in which a student is asked to show that a particular work of art exhibits a style or theme belonging to a certain school or period." More obviously, I give the example of "Presenting legal arguments in front of a judge."

I had found a beautiful example of Scientific writing in an arbitration award written by a Vancouver lawyer named Rod Germaine, in a dispute between an employer and a union regarding call-time pay: the workers had been called out for a shift that was cancelled because a vital piece of machinery in the factory had broken down. The union was demanding four hours' pay for the shift, as specified in the collective agreement. The employer relied on a clause that said they didn't have to pay if the cancellation of the shift was because of circumstances "completely beyond the control" of the employer. So what the arbitrator had to decide was whether the breakdown of the machine was or was not "completely" beyond the company's control.

Mr. Germaine found in favour of the union, because of the word "completely," where most collective agreements he had consulted simply said "beyond the control," without the "completely." To find this particular arbitration ruling, I had pored through many reports published by the Arbitration Branch of the BC Ministry of Labour and so had become quite familiar with the process of an arbitration ruling. Even before Karen Ewing left my office, I was beginning to construct the outer shape of my argument. First I would have a meeting with the College's lawyer and see what facts we could agree on, and then narrow down to the question to be arbitrated. This was going to be fun!

"You can talk with Leo McGrady," Karen said before leaving. "The union will pay for up to four hours of consultation."

This was February, and the arbitration had been scheduled for three days in the first week of July during the summer break. I tucked the matter away and thought I would think about the details and do the research once the semester was over. Back to my classes, and marking papers.

In June, I went up to UBC to consult my helpful colleague Dr. John Dennison in the Faculty of Education. He had made BC's community colleges his speciality, and I thought he might have some useful advice and information for me, and I was right. Dennison pointed me to the International Labour Organization (ILO) which had articulated some principles on the subject of educational leave, and to French law, which states that an employer cannot unreasonably withhold permission for an employee to take leave for any purpose falling under the broad title "improvement of citizenship." The employer has to hold the job open for the employee to return to once his or her leave is over. I was rubbing my hands at the prospect of the upcoming debate. Big shot lawyer on the other side or not, I was assembling some pretty convincing evidence.

I didn't need the four hours with Leo McGrady: half an hour's consultation did the trick.

"Look, Bill," said Leo, "in a case like this you're going to spend most of the three days trying to compare apples and oranges. You'll argue that Malaspina or Camosun College devote a larger percentage of their instructional budget to pay for educational leave than Capilano does, and therefore Capilano should increase the allocation, and the College lawyer will argue back that you have a better dental plan than those colleges; so give up your dental plan and you can have more for educational leave."

"What if we go into the hearing with a table of all benefits at all the colleges, agreed to by both parties?"

Leo spread his hands in surprise. "I think that would be a first in BC!" he said. "You'd be making legal history."

So, next I went to see Marie Jessup, Cap College's extremely brilliant bursar, and told her what I wanted. She listened with an amused smile on her face. "You know what?" she said, when I had finished. "I would actually like that information myself. I should be able to get it from the big computers in Victoria. How soon do you need it?"

A week later, Marie called me to pick up the chart. Her office was right across the way from President Paul Gallagher's office, and I noted that he observed me going in to see Marie.

Marie handed me her table of figures for each of the nine colleges and four institutes in BC. "Will that do?" she asked superfluously. I studied the paper. "It's perfect," I said. "Is the College's lawyer prepared to sign off on this to agree that it's accurate?

She stood up and pushed her office door closed. "The Dean of Instruction, Frank Gelin, has already agreed to sign off on it for the College. So the College's lawyer doesn't need to. Listen," she said, "why even go to arbitration, Bill? Couldn't you and Paul just sit down together and come to an agreement?"

"I'm willing!" I said. "You tell Paul."

I waited half-expectantly for a phone call from Paul Gallagher, but nothing came.

A night or two later, I had a most uncomfortable dream: I was hurrying to embark on a ship, but at the docks I found that construction was taking place, and there were diversions through some plywood-covered channels. As I struggled to make my way from one walkway to another, I could no longer see the ship. When I eventually emerged from the diversion channels, I was in the wrong place, and I could see the ship over to my left, already steaming away from the dock. I sat bolt upright in the bed and said aloud, "Oh shit! I've missed the boat!"

Sharon woke up and I told her my dream.

"It's the ed leave arbitration," she said. "You think you've screwed up somehow."

Sharon's intuitive logic is always dead on. As I sat downstairs drinking coffee, it slowly dawned on me that I had no clear idea of what would happen in the arbitration room. I had simplistically thought of it as a debate: that I would stand up and speak, then the College lawyer would stand up and speak, and then again, and then again, like two schoolboys in front of a teacher, and eventually arbitrator Bruce McColl would retire and make a decision. That's not how it would go at all! The "lawyer" doesn't speak the argument directly; the lawyer questions carefully chosen witnesses. The witnesses do the talking. I had to write a convincing argument using the witnesses' answers as my pen.

I needed to construct my argument like a persuasive essay. Begin with the evidence of how vital ed leaves are to the health of a teaching institution. Begin with a hook perhaps, start out with Bob Sherrin as my witness.

"Mr. Sherrin, do you teach English Composition, English 100?"

"Yes I do. Every semester I teach two sections of English 100."

"And what textbooks do you use for that course?"

Arbitrator interrupts: "Where is this going please, Mr. Schermbrucker."

"You'll see in a moment your Honour. Please be patient. The textbooks, Mr. Sherrin?"

"I use your textbooks, *The Aims and Strategies of Good Writing* and *The Capilano Reader*."

"And do you know how I came to create those two books?"

"Yes. The College's Educational Leave Committee selected your application and you were awarded an ed leave. In order to reduce your rent, on your reduced ed leave salary, you moved to Saturna Island for a year and produced the books."

"Okay. Now I want to establish what value those books have for the College. Do—"

College lawyer: "Objection, your Honour, irrelevant. The value of ed leaves is not in question here. The question at bar is the amount of allocation of funds to ed leaves."

"Mr. Schermbrucker?"

"Your Honour, the dollar amount of allocation to fund ed leaves has a direct connection to the value of the leaves themselves. There may be a public perception that university and college faculty get sabbaticals as a reward for long service, a kind of holiday, and therefore it's a frill that can be cut in times of budget stress. I intend to show that at least at Capilano College, the use made of ed leaves, after rigorous scrutiny by the selection committee has a direct connection to excellence in instruction and to the College's reputation."

And so on, if the arbitrator and my objecting opponent allowed me to get that far.

Then on to the next segment of my argument: asking expert witnesses to interpret some of the documents I submitted, such as the ILO statement of the importance of ed leaves, and the law of France which states that educational leave for the purpose of "improvement of citizenship" is a citizen's right.

I steeled myself to realize that all the documentation I had assembled would be ancillary exhibits. My main job was to ask my expert witnesses carefully crafted questions, and in their replies they would articulate my argument. I went to my office at the College, drew up a list of a dozen witnesses and started phoning them to come and see me. My coup de grace would be calling the bursar as a witness and asking her to interpret the comparative table of benefits at the nine colleges and four institutes.

My phone rang. Marie Jessup: "Bill, I've got the table of data signed off by Frank Gelin in my office, if you want to come and pick it up."

When I got there, I noticed Paul Gallagher was in his office with the door open. After picking up the document from Marie, I couldn't resist knocking on Paul's doorpost, and he invited me in. He was a very cordial man and I had known him since just before his employment at Capilano. When he applied for the president's job (still called principal then), I was on the selection committee, and when his interview was scheduled, I was going to be out of town, so I interviewed him privately in Toronto, where I had gone for a board meeting of the Canadian Periodical Publishers' Association. He sat with me in the lounge of the Delta Chelsea Hotel, and we talked so intensely that neither of us even took a sip out of our beers for a couple of hours. I told him that Capilano College was unique in several ways.

"But none more so than its coordinator system, which does away with ranks and has created a collective of equals, so that the people running the show essentially are the dedicated faculty.

Externally, the administrators deal with government and the public, but internally their role is to facilitate."

He seemed to understand me, and we parted with satisfaction after a good conversation. I voted for him to be principal, which he duly became. Now, sitting in his office, we were possibly adversaries on opposite sides of the arbitration.

"Marie says you and I should sit down and settle the ed leave thing," he said.

"Well, I'm here and sitting in your office, Paul. What is the sticking point?"

"As you well know, we face budget shortfalls every year. Up till now, the College has considered ed leave funds soft funds, so we've had to cut the allocation vertically when necessary, if you speak that language?"

"Yes I know, a vertical cut takes the whole column out. Horizontal cuts take a percentage off each allocation, but don't destroy one allocation column completely."

"Right. We understand one another. Now, we're prepared to say that ed leave is important enough that it should not be cut vertically. Our problem is the disparity between the needs of, say, an Art History instructor who needs to spend a whole year in the art galleries and studios of Florence at 60% of salary, and, say, a Welding instructor who needs a week's ed leave to attend an intensive upgrading course in Kamloops. He needs—welding instructors are usually men—about 150% of salary just for that one week to cover his motel and meals, plus funds to pay his or her replacement here for that week. And the Vocational instructors won't need many such leaves."

"We should be able to figure this out, Paul! You've got a doctorate and so do I."

"Where are you going to be tomorrow?"

"In my office in Humanities, interviewing witnesses."

When I came in on Saturday morning, as I signed in to be admitted by a uniformed security guard, I noticed that Paul had already signed in—unnecessarily, because I knew he had keys to pretty much everything in the College. He wanted me to see his signature and know he was there.

As I finished with a witness, I saw Paul strolling past my window, and I beckoned him into Humanities and we sat together in the Silent Study. "Here's my problem, Bill," Paul said and proceeded to repeat himself from the day before about the different circumstances affecting Vocational instructors versus Academic and Career division instructors.

"So what's the blockage, Paul?"

"I'm not prepared to allocate 1 or 2 or 3% of instructional budget on a regular basis so that Vocational instructors can sit around for a whole year doing nothing on 60% salary. They need that intense week at 150%."

How many Vocational courses were we actually offering? I wondered. I vaguely remembered that there was a Front End Maintenance course given at our Squamish campus. I didn't quite know what Front End Maintenance was, but it obviously had to do with vehicles—lubricating the steering and suspension of cars and trucks? Not clear.

What was *clear* was the political aspect of his conundrum: Paul wanted to treat Vocational instructors differently from Academic and Career instructors. He knew as well as I did that the Faculty Association would never accept such a discrimination.

We talked, and put numbers on bits of paper and pushed them across the table to one another, and at the end of about an hour, we had reached an agreement: The College would allocate 3% of the Academic and Career divisions' instructional budget to ed leaves, and 0.46% of the Vocational division instructional budget. But when it came to applications for ed leave all members were equal, in that anybody could apply for any kind of leave at any variable rate. It would be up to the Ed Leave Committee to sort out the complexities and select who got a leave and at what rate.

It was a messy compromise on both sides, but if we had ed leaves designated as hard money, not subject to vertical cutting, that was a step forward. The disparity between instructors in the three different divisions could wait for another collective agreement negotiation.

Paul held his hand across the table and I shook it. We then retired to separate offices to call our principals. The matter was settled.

Damn! Now I would not get my day in court! All the research I had done would go into a filing cabinet or a box or be chucked out. But that was just a small disappointment. To have settled the arbitration before it went to the arbitrator was a great victory for me.

"Congratulations!" Karen Ewing said when I phoned. "I knew you could do it!"

"That sounds good," Ed Lavalle said on the phone. "Bring the paper in and let's look at it."

"Are you driving down the hill?" Paul asked, when he came back from talking to his "language people."

I drove him down to a service station to pick up his car, and he slipped into the same private mode we had shared together in Toronto when I interviewed him for the principal's job. He told me he had to have a new car every two years and always properly serviced; I told him I did my own servicing and didn't care if the car was new or old. I noticed his fingernails were overgrown and not well groomed. They had ragged ends. I wondered what his private life was like. I wondered if he too would go home and announce a victory to his family over the supper table.

I need not have worried about losing my day in court. A couple of years after this, in October 1983, Vancouver had its Solidarity rally, to protest against the "new reality" of austere funding cuts to all kinds of public services announced by Premier Bill Bennett's Social Credit government. The Faculty Association advised that it was up to individual instructors whether or not to cancel class and attend the rally or allow our students to attend. I don't know what concrete achievements came from the rally, but it was huge, a landmark event in Vancouver's history, with estimates of 40,000 to 50,000 marching through the streets. Union Leader Jack Munro negotiated a settlement with Premier Bennett, which some called a victory and others a sellout.

After the Solidarity rally, at Capilano College a memo went out from the administrators to all department coordinators asking them to report the names of all faculty who had cancelled classes because of the rally. Most if not all coordinators refused.

A year later, on Monday 6th August 1984, the Capilano Faculty Association, a registered trade union, received a letter from Principal Paul Gallagher, announcing that the College was making improvements to its administration structure, by creating ten new administrative positions of "director." The letter came to me as the union's Corresponding Secretary, and when I read the first paragraph aloud at an executive meeting, there was a stunned silence. Then Ed Lavalle, our Chief Steward, said: "TEN directors? What the hell are they going to do? Read the rest of it, please."

The second paragraph invited faculty to apply for the new director positions as they were phased in over the next year or two. And the third paragraph mentioned, as though it was an afterthought, that there would be fewer release sections needed in future for coordinators.

"Well that's pretty damn clear," Ed said. "They're announcing that they want to take the coordinators out of the bargaining unit and make them into administrative servants who will do whatever they're told. We'll have to stop this."

"Look at the date," I said. "Hand delivered to me on Monday 6th August—when the faculty are just beginning to come back from summer holidays. Does Paul think he can slip this through on us?"

So began the biggest resistance effort the union had ever made. We had fought other fights, mostly for women instructors, trying to get part timers onto the benefits train in less than ten years, but now, Paul Gallagher was trying to mess with founding Dean of Instruction Les Brooks' collegial model based on coordinators as functional officers within the departments, rather than hierarchical heads.

Paul could not have chosen a worse fight. It went on for a couple of years and ended in the Labour Relations Board. The Vice-chairman of the LRB hearing our case took another year to make his ruling, which was that he didn't need to make a ruling because the matter could be arbitrated under the collective agreement.

Perhaps the tipping point came when 474 faculty put their

signatures to a double-page centrefold ad in the *North Shore News*, under the heading in 36-point type:

TO THE BOARD OF GOVERNORS
OF CAPILANO COLLEGE:

COME TO YOUR SENSES!

Writing as an individual faculty member, not the union's corresponding secretary, I sent a personal letter to each member of the Board by name, pointing out that there was a fatal illogicality in their press explanations that in order to determine which classes should be cut, under budget restraints, it was necessary to hire ten new administrators. "We don't have enough money, so we have to sink a lot of ships, so let's hire more admirals?" I taunted them.

I'll say this for Paul Gallagher: he had the humility and good sense to know when he was beaten. The union declared the director positions hot, and only one faculty scab applied and was appointed a director. Pretty soon she disappeared to a job elsewhere. After our double-page spread in the *North Shore News*, after our frustrating days in the Labour Relations Board, Paul quietly phased out his ill-conceived directors plan, and then he himself went on to become president of Langara College.

Looking back on it, I now wonder if the intense sit-down Paul and I had in the Delta Chelsea Inn in Toronto, where I explained to him how the coordinator system was the very heart of Capilano College, might perhaps have had the exact opposite effect on him than I thought it had. I thought he was listening to me and adjusting himself mentally to fit in. Maybe not. Maybe even at that early moment, he was resolving that he would change all that and put his own mark on the College.

In the Labour Relations Board hearings, Crawford Kilian, the Communications Department Coordinator testified that at a department party, Dean (later President) Greg Lee got into a discussion with some faculty about the directors plan and eventually stated frankly, "The College needs people it can fire." Oh, so did the frustration of having the coordinators refuse to report the Solidarity absences lead Paul to try converting them all into directors?

In 1990, I was invited to be the keynote speaker at a Capilano College coordinators retreat on Vancouver Island. Retreats of this sort have been a feature of Capilano College since the beginning. Originally arranged by Dean Les Brooks on a regular basis, they were a chance to escape from the pressures of the campus for two or three days and go to some neutral and congenial place, and talk and think outside the box. The token payment for my participation at the retreat at the Qualicum Inn was a coffee mug which sits treasured on my desk today.

The system which Principal Alf Glenesk and Dean Les Brooks put in place, the coordinator system of departmental administration, was the key to what Capilano College became. Collegiality means things take a lot of talking out. It is a delicate balance. In the short run, it's inefficient. In the long run, it's incomparable. Many times I have heard complaints from departmental support staff (formerly called secretaries, but now called more appropriately divisional assistants and learning assistants) that it takes so long to break the new coordinators in. That's true, but the steady rotation of faculty through the roles of running the department makes for a more creative, congenial and informed department.

The essential transaction in any school is the transaction

between teacher and student. Everything that enhances those meetings of minds is good; anything that gets in the way, distracts, or moves resources to other functions is misguided.

* * *

And a couple of years after the big directors' fight at Capilano, here I sit in Kenya with my big old farmer friend David Stanley, talking in his little farm house. Dave is listening to my campus battles back in North Vancouver, while his eyes stray up the dry hillside as he desperately tries to figure out how to keep his cattle alive through yet one more year of drought by maybe grinding up *acacia* and *leleshwa* bushes into feed.

Eventually his gaze returns to me and he says, "So, you don't really have any problems then! Just a question of who gives the orders?"

"Something like that," I concede for the time being.

THE ANATOMY OF TEXTBOOK WRITING AT CAPILANO

JOHN SAYRE

I BEGAN TEACHING economics at Capilano College as its doors opened in the fall of 1968 (I was, technically, the first faculty member hired but my hat is off to Bill Schermbrucker who was the first *full-time* faculty member at the institution).

Teaching the discipline that I had come to love was not a big challenge since the "right" way to present both the micro and the macro principles was subject to only minor disagreements across a wide spectrum of economists and there were only three or four textbook choices—all American publications that had been "Canadianized"—a reality that hardly seemed to matter since the majority of those teaching the courses in BC's new colleges and at SFU were Americans (myself included).

But the world changed and things ceased to be so simple. As all who lived through the 1970s surely recall, the world's economies experienced a decade of turmoil and unprecedented confusion. Inflation hit levels previously thought to be the exclusive purview of Latin American economies.

An interesting spinoff of this was Prime Minister Trudeau imposing price controls on Thanksgiving Day (!), 1975, barely one year after he won the federal election by opposing Stanfield's proposal to do what *he* had just done. But far more significantly, unemployment rates around the globe were *rising* along with the runaway inflation. Standard macro economic theory said that this could not happen, and the discipline was in chaos. Furthermore, governments were at a loss as to how to react to rising inflation and rising unemployment.

By the mid-1980s the world's economies had settled back into more "normal" levels of inflation and unemployment, and macro economic theory had experienced a revolution of sorts.

Despite the sense of returning to normal, I gradually came to realize that the 1970s had led me to an evolution of uneasy feelings about what was going on in the classrooms of this country.

The focus of this uneasiness was three-fold. First, I felt that in the face of the revolution in macroeconomic thought, "the system" was demanding way too much of the student who was just beginning to learn this fascinating discipline. The proverbial straw here occurred one early spring day in 1990 when I received the latest edition of the most popular text on the market. I was aware of the trend towards longer texts but this one floored me. I quickly looked at the back of the book and "sucked air" when I saw the number 1,260 on the last page. I held it in my hands and moved my arms up and down a little—as one might do in trying to decide whether a chicken was big enough to feed all of us. Next, I walked down to the physics lab on the 3rd floor of the Fir building to weigh the book. It was 6.1 pounds!

I asked myself: how many first / second year students are going to slug their way through one thousand plus pages and six pounds of economics in their pursuit of learning "the principles" of the discipline? For that matter, how many instructors are going to cover even one half of this text in a 13–15 week semester? I had a definite sense of things, having edged beyond the absurd, now hurtling into the very core of Wonderland.

The second concern had a political flavour to it. No principles of economics text that I had ever seen in this country had pointed out that what might well be "good economic policy" in the context of a huge economy with minimal imports and whose currency was *the* international standard (the US and its dollar) might not be such good policy in the context of a small economy which imported a great deal and had a flexible exchange rate—the Canadian case. Why had none of the Canadian economists who "converted" the American texts into the appearance of not being American picked up on this point? (This is but one example of many possible examples of a political naïveté I perceived among most Canadian economists.)

The third concern was the one that really got my blood boiling. While it is true that the stagflation of the 1970s had exposed a limitation in Keynesian analysis that had so cleanly and clearly explained the policy blunders of the Great Depression, it was also true that the Keynesian analytical model was still a powerful tool that greatly helped students learn essential relationships in macroeconomics.

Yet in the 1980s we began to see the rise of a group of economists who had a self-righteous and condescending attitude towards Keynesian economics wrapped up in the resurgence of Neo-Classical thought that took us back between 60 and 150 years in time. The possible consequences of this were, in my view, beyond irritating—they were frightening. The ideological tone of the young radicals who embraced all aspects of "free market economics" seemed to be saying that we should ignore the lessons that were so brutally taught us by the severity and length of the lost decade of the 1930s.

All of this culminated in my saying something to the effect: "The hell with it, I will do it *right*, myself."

In the summer of 1991 I had shifted into high gear. I had a beautiful place to work in the Fir building—4th floor, corner office with sets of windows on both the east and south sides. It was bright, strangely quiet and the scent of heavily-forested air was but a breath away. I would get in to the office by 7:00 if not earlier (the first staff person arrived about 8:25) and would stay until dark—9:00 or even 10:00 in the month of June.

I remember thinking on the long walk to the empty north campus parking lot one evening that I might as well live in the Fir building. This thought proved to be prophetic the next summer when I did, in fact, live in the building for several weeks while digging myself out of financial disaster brought on by divorce and $40,000-a-year University of Chicago tuition, among other things.

By the fall of 1992 I had produced five chapters of the macro text when two significant turning points occurred. First, I asked my colleagues to give what I had done so far a quick read and some feedback. An excited Alan Morris—our most recent hire in the department—got back to me very quickly. He made it explicitly clear that he had to be in on this project since my approach to economics and my Platonic-dialogue writing style were so much like his own. (I did not know that he actually had the start of a micro text in his office at the time. In fact, I learned of this only when he gave me feedback on the piece of writing you are currently reading).

Second, I had been greatly encouraged by a conversation with a senior editor from McGraw-Hill who had sought me out for "exploratory talks" on one of her trips to the west coast. (I will never forget that my 12-year-old daughter and I drove to a West End hotel to meet Jennifer for what I assumed to be a half-hour, one at the most, meet-up early one Thursday evening. The very bright, fast-talking editor from Toronto and I sat across the table from each other for nearly four hours! Meridith, my youngest daughter, was very patient and quiet the whole time—something I can only marvel about now.)

My initial reaction to Alan was one of great caution. I had just come out of a series of joint ventures to make money with "friends" and they had all crashed quite badly. At that point I said to myself: from here on out I will do it (everything, anything) myself.

But, on the other hand I had worked for quite a while already and had less than one half of one of the two texts needed to comprise a set to compete with the likes of Lipsey, Samuelson, and Baumol. In the end, the scale of what I had bitten off and my impressions of Alan's character won out and we agreed to a 50% joint effort and reward.

The partnership was launched by early 1992 and a pattern of work quickly emerged. We were both full-time instructors with children and busy lives. (Also, one or the other of us was the Commerce Program coordinator during the span from inception to 2005.) But we also knew that continuous effort towards specific goals was needed to actually finish what we had set out to do.

Every Friday we would both arrive before 9:00 a.m. exchanging the greetings: "Good morning, captain" with "Good morning, squire," and go off to our respective offices for intense work until at least 4:30 in the afternoon (no lunch break). As day's end approached, we would sit together, talk over the upcoming week in terms of teaching, exams, committee work and personal life, and then agree to precisely what we wanted finished in exactly one week.

We would squeeze in bits and pieces of time during the week

but if we began the next Friday "behind schedule" we faced a very intensive several hours to finish by day's end—or face coming in on Saturday / Sunday to finish. In short, we both realized that it was going to take an enormous amount of effort and that there simply was no room for down time.

A productive summer of 1992 resulted in our being in high gear by the start of the 1992 / 93 academic year. Then on March 30, 1993 we signed a contract with McGraw-Hill Ryerson, setting out a series of deadlines that culminated in both books being completed by March of 1995—two years to produce two 13-chapter textbooks (one macro and one micro) with a built-in study guide for each of the 26 chapters, the answer key for students, an instructor's manual with answer key for the unanswered questions in the text, and a computerized test bank with at least 100 multiple-choice questions for each chapter (100 times 26 equals 2,600 questions).

Oh my God!

In the summers of 1993 and 94, the two professional-development months (May and August) plus most of the other two summer months were devoted full time to the book. It was during this time that differences in our work patterns became apparent. Alan worked more intensely that I did but for shorter periods, while I was slower—more prone to take a little break—but stayed at my desk later into the evening. This difference in approach was no problem as long as each of us finished our specific work on the immediate goal (usually a chapter) on schedule.

Were there periods of doubt about whether we would finish? Not many, but I do remember one in particular. In the summer of 1993 individual faculty did have computers in their offices but the routine of getting something printed meant putting one's file on a floppy disk and taking it to the print shop in the basement of the Arbutus building on the south campus—which, of course, was open only normal business hours of the five-day work week. By now, Alan and I were often working late into the evening and on weekends and needed access to the print shop when it was closed.

We took our dilemma about how to get stuff printed quickly during odd hours to (Assistant?) Dean Bill Gibson and, to our delight, he agreed to give us a key to his own office in the Arbutus building that had a *stand-alone printer* (a novel piece of technology that would become commonplace in less than a decade). He then had the computer support people hook our computers to his printer.

Thus, printing for us became hitting the print command on our computers in the Fir building and then walking down to the Arbutus building to pick up the pages. I clearly remember many frustrating times when I would be standing in the Arbutus building with the computer printout in my hand, speaking on the phone to Alan, who was in the Fir building, about the particular way(s) that what we had just tried to do had not worked. Often, I would have to run back up with the printout and the two of us would try to figure out what to do to make it fit the page—or whatever—then change it, hit the print command and then run back down to Arbutus to get the printed page.

Yes, there were times when doubt about finishing did creep into my mind while gazing up at those intimidating four flights of stairs in the Fir building once again holding the most recent printout that obviously needed more editing which, of course, would mean yet more trips up those long stairs.

As an amusing aside to this story, I just now recalled how Alan and I would always take Dean Gibson's wastebaskets out to the bin behind the building each night / weekend and empty them for fear that if he saw how much paper we were using (and thus the number of copies done) the deal might be off.

We had obtained a contract from McGraw Hill by selling the McGraw-Hill editor on our ability to deliver a set of material that would be guided by four clear goals:

a) produce two well-written texts that spoke directly to the student;

b) stay focused on essential time-honoured principles that would chop in half the current 1000-page-plus approach, which was then the norm of what was available in the market;

c) apply our idea of "students best learn economics by doing economics" by building a complete, carefully thought-out study guide into each chapter; and

d) our commitment to do all the writing of both texts as well as all the other supplementary materials—test banks, instructor's manuals, answer keys, Power Point packages, etc.—ourselves. That would avoid the problem with the current texts, which had serious discontinuities arising from the supplementary materials being farmed out to people other than the primary authors. The result would be, of course, a set of principles texts that were integrated and truly made in Canada.

Identifying time-honoured principles was aided by the fact that the educational beginnings in economics for Alan and for myself were so different—he from a "working-class" university in the midlands of England and I from a private university in the western US. We saw the world quite differently at times, and somehow this enabled us to see the common ground we shared much more easily than either of us had expected.

We quickly adopted the habit (which we continue to follow to this day) that each of us reads *all* of what the other has written, but we do not make even the smallest change without the other's knowledge and consent. This process, I am convinced, greatly aided the result of two well-written books—a description that market feedback has clearly awarded to our books. The process ensured that when either of us would write drivel, the other would surely jump on it and point out that improvement was needed. The study guide was strong from the start and this was aided by Alan's meticulousness and his strong math skills combined with my willingness to not just go outside the box but to throw the damn box away.

When the first draft of macro was complete, we encouraged our colleagues to try it out in the classroom and most were happy to do so. This led to an experience that taught us both a lesson in the importance of appearances. The feedback we got back from one colleague, at the end of the fall semester was: "You guys better not quit your day job." Not an overwhelming word of encouragement.

Then something interesting happened. Since we spent all of the spring semester and all summer on the micro text, we were unable to work on the macro text—except for changing the font, and a few other cosmetic touch-ups such as introducing novel ways to use italics, the bold option and line spacing—things we had learned doing the micro. At the start of the new fall term the same colleague came rushing through the door of my office to congratulate us on the great improvement we had made to the (macro) text and marvel at how hard we must have worked on it. I know of no alternative to silence when one faces this sort of situation.

We got much more useful feedback from the 24 peer reviewers that the publisher had chosen, and the feedback was really quite good. But would it sell?

In the end we met all of the publisher-imposed deadlines and the two books came out early in 1996, just under six years after groundbreaking. A joint effort of McGraw-Hill and the College resulted in a very classy but relaxed book launch party in the faculty lounge on the 4th floor of the Fir building (the same room I had slept in for a few months three years earlier). The reality of what we had done was settling in. But would it sell?

Very soon after we got an indication. An instructor at UBC ordered a thousand copies! Our initial reaction was excitement at such great news, but more thought raised a serious issue. McGraw-Hill had positioned the two texts as the fresh new approach that would fly under the radar of the big university-focused texts—a product that was shorter, better written, student-friendly, coming out of a Canadian college and flowing back into many Canadian colleges. In fact, they had hoped Sayre and Morris would sweep the colleges in Ontario and English-speaking Quebec—and the first adoption was the biggest university in the west. Was the market going to perceive Sayre and Morris as another entry in a horse race we didn't want to run? It was with relief that several colleges did pick up Sayre and Morris in the next few weeks and we were launched.

Within a year the question of whether Sayre and Morris would go into a second edition or end up being a one-shot affair was a debate within McGraw-Hill. This is always an issue with a new text in a market as small as Canada: How much money is a publisher prepared to lose to keep a new text visible long enough to overcome the natural inertia in the market? The truth is that most instructors would rather stick with the text they are using than have to write a whole new set of notes to accommodate a new one.

Alan and I never got any details but it appears that a young, hard-working and eager junior editor argued that she could make us an ongoing winner if she could take over and be given a budget to go four-colour. Not knowing the outcome of this debate caused tension with Alan and me, and we prepared ourselves for bad news.

But the news carried us enthusiastically into the rush of another edition and perhaps much more after that. In the two years that we worked on the second edition, we began to see the most rewarding and genuine form of flattery—imitation. The competitor texts coming onto the market were shorter in length and imitated several of our little innovations. For example, our practice of identifying and then defining necessary economics jargon when it was first used was copied, as was our addition of sections on chapter summaries and student study tips.

The peer reviews on the first edition that we were getting back raised the issue of should we stick with using the Keynesian model in the macro text or bend to what appeared to be the growing popularity of the supply-side approach. It was not lost upon us that this also meant deciding to stay with what is perceived to be liberal, left-wing ideas or join the growing numbers on the growing conservative side.

Alan and I did not (and do not) have the same political view of the world, but this never created any ongoing problems between us simply because we were both convinced that any good principles text should explain the conflicting views within the discipline as well as we knew how and leave it to the student to sort which of the presented views was "right"—if that was important to them.

Nonetheless, we were using the Keynesian model and a quick glance at the table of contents would reveal that to any knowledgeable economist. Furthermore, we knew that the anti-Keynesian sentiment was so strong that we would lose adoptions if we continued with our approach. Nonetheless, we stuck to our guns because somewhere down deep, we both believed that Keynes offered a valid model for understanding the whole of the macro economy while newly presented alternatives, perhaps better in some specific ways, lacked the broad overview. For a while, we were the only "Keynesian text" on the market.

Once the Sayre / Morris principles texts were well enough established to ensure continuity, Alan set up a lunch between us and, before the food even reached the table, proposed that we write another book. The theme would be the idea that through time and across cultural / political frontiers, societies always structure their economies using some blend of the four C's—cooperation, custom, command and competition. It took me a couple of days but I agreed to join and out of it came The *Worlds of Economics* by Morris and Sayre. Once this was on the shelf, Morris and Sayre then produced *Why Economies Fail*. Both of these books are aimed at a more general audience than first- or second-year students and are available on *Amazon.com* and currently used at Capilano University.

And what is the prospect of our efforts? Well, it is certainly true that the tide was turned by the financial crisis of 2008–10 and the subsequent economic recession. The open warfare between the liberal Neo-Keynesians and the conservative Neo-Classicalists has tipped considerably towards the Keynesians, and Sayre and Morris will be very well positioned to offer its 8th edition in the spring of 2015. The two Morris and Sayre books sell a few copies each month and are, to some extent, timeless, so why not many more years of chugging along?

Was it all worth it? Yes.

Could I have done it myself? No.

And we would like to express our gratitude to Capilano University as an institution and to our colleagues, past and present, for giving us support through it all.

THE CAP I KNEW

BILL MURDOCH

I CONSIDER MYSELF exceptionally fortunate to have had the privilege of working with students at Capilano College for thirty-one years prior to retirement. To be paid to share my understanding of the arts of acting, theatre and film was something for which I remain eternally grateful.

Beyond my own infatuation with the subject matter and the joys and challenges of teaching new groups of young people each year, was the atmosphere of the place itself. I came as a temporary fresh out of a master's program at UBC, hired to help establish theatre courses and resources. The aim as I understood it was to create credible offerings for students under the banner of the Humanities Division.

The English department was a prime mover in that desire, and the unique collegial decision-making model allowed departments the independence to manage the resources allotted them as they saw fit. As the largest department under the Division of Humanities, English had a great deal of say, but this was always after consultation with all members of faculty.

At the time I was hired, the Humanities Division consisted of Modern Languages (French and Spanish), Philosophy, Fine Arts, English and the fledgling—Theatre. A Theatre course had been offered through English's allotment of course sections, and it was their desire that a group of more practical courses should develop as a complement to academic study of theatre literature.

It was due to their initial push that the present extensive offerings of Theatre, Film and Musical Theatre got their start. This was an initiative from the ground up, made possible by the College model and the enshrining in contract language by the Faculty Association of the principles of group decision-making. I came to realize, as I sat in department meetings, how immediate and personal was the impact of Humanities decisions, on my continuing employment and the employment of my colleagues around the table. I came in a time of plenty; there was funding for extra sections so the table could afford to be generous to me and my colleague Dawn Moore.

As the newest temporary employee, I was only too conscious that if we didn't maintain class maximums as close to 100% as possible, our sections, and in particular my sections, would be reassigned. I was allowed to argue in person to both my coordinator and our division chair at that same table for the need for keeping class maximums to 20 when the others at the table were teaching 33 per section. I could also argue for the rental of Presentation House Theatre once a year to showcase our work and explain why we needed spaces to build sets and have a dedicated space to teach our studio courses.

These were expensive items at the time, but I was fortunate in having sympathetic colleagues, coordinators and chairs who took our case forward to the administration. When appropriate for the College as a whole, those spaces were funded and we were finally able to move into R Building along with the bookstore. On reflection, I now see that the collegial model in this instance was not only efficient in terms of maximizing the resources of the Humanities Division, but also pedagogically very sound: we ended up with a space that worked exceptionally well for our needs. We could make our voices heard, and decisions—which may have taken longer to reach—when implemented came off very smoothly. This I feel was due to the political structure outlined above.

The other aspects of the College that I found particularly gratifying were the human scale of the place and the dedication of faculty and staff to the shared aims of the institution. It was dedicated to teaching as its raison d'etre and therefore it attracted the best of teachers. We had to have a strong practical background in our respective fields and a down-to-earth approach. We knew we could expect a diverse group of students—some coming back after years of work, some just out of high school and wanting to dabble in many disciplines but not willing to sit in huge classrooms to do so, and still others needing a bit more personalized attention due to special challenges.

At Cap they could cope and indeed were welcomed to the "disability friendly" place that Cap prided itself on being. The notion of being a "place of higher learning"—a university—a remote "Cloud Cuckoo Land"—was absent. The College system was very enlightened.

The human scale mentioned above very much manifested itself for me in my role as producer for the Cap Theatre Productions. I needed to get shows on with part-time students, so time was of the essence. I had to go from dean's office to chair's office to get budgets approved, the Media Production Centre to get promotional material done, the mailroom to stuff mailboxes with fliers, Maintenance to get a pick-up to move sets, and the Print Shop to get posters and scripts printed.

All those resources existed and were staffed by people only too willing to help a fledgling Theatre guy. Indeed, it was the openness and willingness of all these people to help, no matter how busy they were, that made our productions as successful as they were. We were even able to enlist the help of the Student Union to co-sponsor our beer gardens when we needed to raise money for a band for one of our shows. That was when you could on a Thursday evening have a beer after class for three bucks. And at that price we were able to employ Mosquito Creek—a bluegrass ensemble of no mean musical abilities (who also played at the fund raiser)—to accompany "Ten Lost Years" for its three-week run at Presentation House.

As a final note, I would just like to add that because of the wonderful start I had at the place on my thirty-one-year teaching journey, Cap will always be for me a college—a place where students come first and where the consultation at all levels resulted in an institution that needed no PR to convince students that it was a great place to learn. They came, and in my case kept my courses full. For that I shall always fondly remember the place for feeding my family and giving me a place to play.

COMING TO CAP

WILL GOEDE

IT WAS THE SUMMER of 1988. I was trying to find a way back to teaching in the Orient when I got a call from Maria Hindmarch, departmental coordinator at Capilano College. My interview had gone well; I had three-fifths of a job at the College starting in the fall. I thought, Wow, a real job! But when I thought about it again, I wasn't sure. What was the College like? Did presidents and vice-presidents and vice-vice presidents run the school and use the Board as a rubber stamp? Did deans and vice deans dominate the curriculum? Was the College just another post-secondary mill?

I was fifty-six at the time, a peripatetic scholar. University of Maine, University of California, University of Victoria, Cariboo College, Malaspina College, Camosun College, the Open University, to name a few. I hadn't felt at home in any but Cariboo. It didn't help matters that some administrators along the way had disapproved of my teaching methods.

Occasionally it had come down to a matter of old allegiances and power politics. At California, for instance, I had to sign a loyalty oath to the State of California. At BC community colleges, with as I said the exception of Cariboo, there had been questionable learning environments and dysfunctional faculty-administration relationships.

Would Capilano be another UVic, where in 1970 I had alarmed the Head of the English department by a kind of subversive "impatience" and "immaturity"? Would Maria Hindmarch one day call me into her office and lecture me about such things?

Would she, like the chairman and the dean at UVic, short-circuit the faculty tenure process and leave the decision up to the president, thereby preventing my being given reasons for denial of tenure and then disallowing due process of appeal?

Disinherited and under-employed, I had been teaching in China and Indonesia since 1982. Both countries were totalitarian regimes, but, curiously, never once had any administrator questioned my educational methods. In both countries students were able and enthusiastic learners. At Chinese universities students admired me because I was obviously a cousin of Bei Quian Daifu, Dr. Norman Bethune, and hence a wise man. At Indonesian universities they listened carefully to everything I said because they wanted to go to Canada and play in the snow.

In spite of deep apprehension, I decided to accept Maria's offer. I would have to rethink my dream of working and perhaps even retiring and living out my life in the storied Far East.

I don't think my teaching methods were "subversive." When I was at UVic, classes were called lectures. You were supposed to lecture students, and they were to sit and listen to you and when called upon, to write down what you said. I had always tried not to do that. It was my way to ask students to take charge of their own learning. Of course, it isn't always easy to learn that way. Better to write everything down and memorize it.

In my classes, however, students soon realized they had to decide what they wanted to learn in the course and how to learn it, and they also had to convince me that they were looking at the materials of the course through their own eyes. For instance, students in my first-year English literature class at Cap read excerpts from Gail Sheehy's book *Passages*, a book that charts the changes we all endure during the five or six stages of life: adolescence, marriage and the twenties, middle life, and so forth, into late life.

The great short stories, poems, and novels in the English language can be seen to illustrate those passages in such a way that students can be voyagers in course materials. They can see that the writings are about them at the present moment and can also act as cushions against the inevitable shocks ahead of them.

Capilano College provided the perfect setting for this kind of learning. I taught there from 1988 to 2000. At that time instructors were generally "non-regular" or "regular." It took two years to be "regularized." The process of regularization included student evaluations of their teachers. I like to think most of the evaluations over my first two years came as a result of the discomfort students felt when taking responsibility for their own education. I received some low scores.

As required, the English department put me under "alert and guidance," and I thought it only right that it be so. It was the students, not the administration, who helped to provide the parameters of tenure, and in the end it was the faculty, not the administration, who set about to evaluate the student responses and the way I taught my classes. I am happy to say that eventually I came through with flying colours.

The College was a happy place in those days, the atmosphere collegial, faculty and administrators working together as a team trying to square the budget with the visions of the North Shore community. Sometime during my first week at the College, Doug Jardine, the College president, came into my office and welcomed me aboard and told me if there was anything I wanted, to be sure to come to him for help.

The project that I remember most at Cap was the occasion of reinventing the jazz curriculum. It was good example of how

Cap worked in those days. I was in the English department, but people knew I was also a jazz musician, so I suppose I was invited to represent the general faculty on the committee; others were John Waters, Dean of Arts; Mike Reveley, Jazz Studies Coordinator; two jazz instructors (I believe Rob McKenzie and Ihor Kukurudza); and our outside professional expert, the great jazz hero Phil Nimmons.

We were given the task of coming up with the best jazz curriculum in Canada, no holds barred, and I think we delivered it. Administrators and faculty took and received, and we dared to dream what would work for all of us. Today, if you ask any jazz enthusiast or professional across Canada, you will know that Capilano Jazz Studies is the premier jazz school in Canada.

WHY I LOVED TEACHING AT CAPILANO COLLEGE

MARIA HINDMARCH

I LOVED TEACHING English at Capilano College 1974–2002 because many of my classes were lively, because my colleagues were up to date in their fields and shared their ideas, because we took meetings seriously, and because it was possible to change things that were not working well.

When I was interviewed for a part-time job I had applied for, someone asked me, "What is your psychic geography?" I don't know if I quoted William Blake or Germaine Greer or asked what sort of question is that because another interviewer interjected and objected. I knew from the lively way that Bill Schermbrucker and Frances Brownell reacted to whatever I said or the question itself that this place accepted different viewpoints and was used to debate. While I was driving home that afternoon, I decided to say "yes" to the full-time job they offered me, even though I knew it meant I, a single parent of a toddler, would write less and mark more.

Democratic. Capilano College was the most democratic place I've worked. This means there were meetings and meetings because we had differences on so many things and wanted to come to consensus. Once a consensus was reached, people—instructors, administrators, students on some smaller but important committees such as budget or parking—stuck with it; plus, we had heard every argument along the way, so we quickly learned how to present positions that we may have previously disagreed with. I did this a few times as coordinator—always presenting the strongest point first.

The classroom. So many. I taught some great classes and some clunkers and even rambunctious ones like the English 103 that had five or six class clowns. I also team taught four different times. I just loved getting discussions going and seeing minds turn open to possibilities, which at Cap College was easy to do. We had great teachers in so many fields—music, philosophy, art history, biology, economics, studio art, geography, sociology, history, music, math, languages, chemistry, physics, business, political science, etc.

Students would come from these classes to mine with ideas and experiences just at a stage that their minds were opening to the possibilities of life. I believe some eighteen- to twenty-year-olds can pick up in a month or so concepts and things they may have missed during two years or more of schooling simply because they are now ready. Some transformations simply amazed me.

Some minds too. An example: I woke up at 1:30 a.m. one night and could not get back to sleep. By 2:00 I decided I might as well turn on the light and mark papers in bed. I made my way through commenting on seven of them from my second-year Canadian Literature class when I came upon one that was so good I could not believe it. I wrote comments in the margins and at the end but decided I would have to leave the grade until the next day because I could only give it A++ or 100%, and English teachers don't just do that.

I went to sleep for a couple of hours; then, once I got to the College, I reread Miki Hood's paper on Timothy Findley's *The Wars*. It was as good as I had thought it was in the middle of the night. I gave it to three other teachers to read: full marks. I even sent a copy off to Findley, who replied that he'd like to meet Miki the next time he was in Vancouver. (I assumed she might get a PhD in English; John Dixon, her philosophy prof, said she would get a PhD in philosophy. She chose psychology.)

English 100. Sometimes I had great ones and other times clunkers which I had to work to turn around before anyone could learn anything. Jean Clifford and I would often share our exasperations about clunkers over tea and laugh about what we were trying to do; then (somewhere around the 3rd to 5th week) one of us would get a breakthrough and a week later the other.

One of my favorite moments occurred in a night class just as I was introducing the research paper. I told the class we would look at how to document first. I would show them how they could acknowledge any source whether they were quoting or summarizing or paraphrasing it. I gave them each a journal, a magazine, or a portion of that day's newspaper and asked them to introduce and cite a direct quotation.

"Why do we have to do this?" asked a student. "What's the use?" Another student, I think his name was Mark, stood up and said in booming voice, "I'll tell you why. I have four years at SFU, a degree in science, and this is the most useful course I have ever taken. I only wish I had taken it first before *all* the others." The class immediately went to work. I later found out from Mark that he was in my class because he wanted to take Education at UBC to teach high-school science. UBC would not let him in until he had passed two English courses. Since he lived in Deep Cove, he came to Cap. (From the outset, SFU had no compulsory English requirement for a degree.)

Capilano College then took meetings seriously. Probably still does. We had Instructional Board meetings at the end of the afternoon that often did not end until 6:00 p.m. On Tuesdays, we had department meetings once a month, divisional meetings once a month, Faculty Association meetings twice a month during a two-hour time block in the middle of the day, but if we had not reached consensus then we would have to meet in the middle of Thursday (which happened fairly often) or on a rare 5th Tuesday.

Thursdays were supposed to be held aside for smaller meetings: one of these was the Principal's Advisory Committee. One year I was elected to the Principal's Advisory Committee along with two other members of the Faculty Association, Charles Priester from Business Administration and Art Pape from Media Resources. On the administration side there were three deans plus Peter Spratt, the principal, as chair. He asked the committee to answer planning questions about the next two years, and we asked him to let us see the budget first. He agreed and said he would bring the figures to the next meeting. He didn't do it. He again asked us to plan. We again refused and again he promised the figures.

When he turned up late to the third meeting without the budget, the other administrators looked dismayed. I was furious. Art Pape was too. I couldn't see Charles' eyes but I knew. Art asked for a caucus of the faculty. We retired to an adjoining classroom and wrote a motion of censure that we brought back. I moved it, Art seconded, and we voted for it. The deans abstained. We sent it to the College Board, and within days the principal was no longer with us.

Capilano College was a great place to work for many reasons. Lively debates. Faculty who cared. We shared ideas and frustrations and supported each other. We talked with students wherever we met them, and with each other. We chose our own books and had a great bookstore manager, Bill Zienty. We developed our own outlines and curricula. We could be contemporary: one year I taught Carol Shields' *The Stone Diaries* to a Canadian Literature class in the spring just three weeks before it won the Governor's General's Award for fiction; then I taught it in the fall in an American Literature class just days before it received the Pulitzer Prize.

We identified weaknesses and ways to address them: e.g., the English Placement Test was developed first at Capilano before the name was taken over, later to be renamed the Language Proficiency Index; the Writing Centre, which helps all levels of students and is staffed by several faculty (.5 of a section) not just one or two full-timers as such centres are elsewhere; instructional skills workshops for faculty. We had some excellent counsellors to whom I could take a troubled student for help and who gave us workshops on anger and on harassment. We had lively faculty who were intelligent and knowledgeable in their fields.

When it came to interviewing for new faculty, the English department committee would make up new questions to ask each round of candidates. At least, we did this for a number of years. We went largely on our instincts. If the candidate's voice was monotonous, we wouldn't hire him or her. If we were bored, we knew the students would be. If the instructor wanted to teach only literature classes, we didn't want her or him.

One of the questions I made up was, "What do you do when you have two or three disruptive students at the back of the class?" When Bill and I were on a committee interviewing someone who was then in her twenties and is still teaching at Capilano, she said: "I used to be a lifeguard. I'd just go over to where they are and stand by them and continue on the class." We both looked at each other across the table: yes, we want her.

COMPUTING SCIENCE AT CAPILANO

TAMARA DAKIC

As a part of the April 2013 cuts, the administration of Capilano University suspended the Computing Science department without any consultation with the university community. The Computing Science department was serving the students across campus, from Business to Jazz, and its suspension left a huge void in educational opportunities at Cap. The department has a rich and interesting history at Cap that should not be forgotten.

The first Computing Science course at Cap was taught in 1969, just one year after Capilano College was established. The instructor was Peter Palffy, who was at that time a graduate student in physics at UBC and now is a professor of chemical physics at Kent State University in Ohio. Since at that time Cap didn't have a computer, the instructor took the students to UBC on Saturdays to use the mainframe computer there. The programming language taught was Fortran; punched cards and card readers were used to enter the student programs into the mainframe.

In 1974, Capilano College started a Business Computing program and bought its first computer, an HP 3000. The choice of HP 3000, attributed to Peter Spratt, was controversial since other educational institutions were buying DEC machines. The HP 3000 belonged to a new generation of machines called minicomputers, and it did not require punched cards to program. Instead you could communicate with it through terminals which had keyboards and screens.

Ten such terminals were purchased at the cost of $5000 each and the computer itself was about $400,000. The cost of this cutting-edge technology would be over $1.5 million in today's dollars. The computer had 256K of RAM and a 5MB hard drive; it was also used for student registration by Greg Lee, who at that time was a physics instructor, but later became president of Capilano University.

With a new computer on campus, other instructors, particularly the ones from Math and Physics, decided that computing science courses should be offered to the general student population. The courses had to use Basic for the programming language, since HP 3000 came with it and it would have been too expensive to purchase a licence for Fortran, which would have been the instructors' language of choice.

As the demands on the computer grew, disagreements arose about the priorities on its time. The problem was solved in a typical Capilano College way—a Computer Users Committee that included all interested parties was formed to jointly come up with a solution. As they often were in Cap's collegial culture, the problems were resolved.

In 1984 the Computing Science department was created at Cap, because a new two-year career program called SCAT (Scientific Computing Applications Technology) was launched. The program was very ambitious and progressive at the time. An industry advisory committee was formed that included many industry leaders such as Werner Dettwiler of MacDonald Dettwiler. It was decided that the program should have a very strong academic component, especially in math, but also a lot of practical courses such as programming in Pascal and a course on databases.

Two new Computing Science faculty were hired to teach these courses, but the hiring was not too successful because there were no other Computing Science faculty to do the hiring. Although the program filled very quickly, the College had a student uprising on their hands before the end of the first semester, since the students, quite a lot of them mature students with previous degrees, were extremely unhappy with their Computing Science instruction. Math and Physics instructors who had previously taught Computing Science courses jumped in, and the program was saved. At the same time, more Computing Science courses were offered to non-program students and the department started to grow.

The height of the department was reached during the dot-com era of the late 1990s. The era brought joyous challenges to the department—it couldn't keep up with the demand for courses. The wait lists were huge. Between 1999 and 2004 a new faculty member was hired nearly every term. The popularity of Computing Science during that time brought a different outlook to education. It became clear to the members of the Computing Science department (and likely many other faculty members) that every student should be given the opportunity to participate in this booming new field. At the beginning of the 21st century, new first-year courses that would cover a wide range of student interests and abilities were created, so any student could be given a stepping stone to the field.

In the spring of 2004 the first offering of COMP 106: Programming With Robots was taught. In this introductory programming course, Lego Mindstorm robots were used to illustrate the fundamental concepts in computer programming and problem-solving. Students got a chance to explore robotics and computing science in a fun and stimulating way. Working on small group projects each week, students learned not only the fundamentals of computing science, but also some upper-level concepts such as multithreading (i.e., coordinating two smaller programs that run at the same time). The focus on robotics, and the relationship between hardware and software made this course a natural and effective preparatory course for engineering students in our Engineering Transition Diploma program. In 2008, Capilano College was the first Canadian institution to join MIT's OpenCourseWare initiative, and COMP 106 was offered as an "open" course, freely available to anyone in the world.

In the spring of 2006 the first offering of COMP 165: Multimedia and the Internet was taught. In this course students learned programming through web applications. Due to its immediately practical nature (everyone needs a website!), this course became popular with students from all programs, such as Jazz Studies, where students learned to build websites that they could use to market and sell their music.

Finally, in the fall of 2007 came the first offering of COMP 107: Animated 3D Game Programming. In this course students were introduced to programming using Alice. Alice was developed at Carnegie Mellon University by Randy Pausch (you may have heard his inspiring Last Lecture that as of today has over 16 million views on Youtube) and his team. It eliminated the need for the strict syntax of programming languages, which most novices find overwhelming, in order to focus on more abstract aspects of computer programming. This course was very effective. In an anonymous evaluation, a student wrote: "This is the course for which I worked the least, but learned the most."

In response to a shortage of skilled labour in a number of areas including computing science, in 2004 the B.C. government created a program called "Double the Opportunities," which doubled the number of available seats for (amongst other programs) computing science students at the big BC universities. Unfortunately the timing of this program was not ideal, since it came out just after the dot-com bust, when the perception of demand for computing scientists was down, leading to the demand for computing science programs to decrease as well. So not only were more students enrolling directly into first-year computer science at the big universities, the demand for these programs was on a downturn.

As a result, in 2005 our second-year offerings were cut due to low enrollment. However, during this time a feedback loop was created. Quite a few students came back to Cap from the big universities because of their appreciation for our dedicated teachers and small classes.

As at this time there was a wide range of first-year Computing Science courses at Cap, the faculty, supported by students, started working tirelessly on rebuilding the program. They believed that the demand for computing scientists would inevitably increase once the tech sector started to boom again, but also that every student should have the opportunity not only to discover computing science, but to develop crucial problem-solving and computational thinking skills that they can apply in their lives, regardless of what they end up doing. Indeed, computing science is having an increasing impact on just about every other discipline, especially in the sciences. So the faculty continued to innovate.

The year 2005 brought a lot of sadness to the Computing Science department. Eliza Kuttner, a longtime department member and coordinator, was killed in a nighttime landslide in her house on Chapman Way in North Vancouver. At the time of her death, Eliza was working on a proposal to run a summer robotics camp for girls in Grades 5 and 6. The proposal, finished by the other faculty members and submitted to the University of British Columbia's Jade Bridges Initiative for promoting efforts to increase the participation of women in science and engineering across British Columbia and the Yukon, was successful and the camp ran in July 2005.

The field of computing science is changing so rapidly that even the courses that had been taught for years underwent a complete makeover every few years. Every makeover not only brought new technologies to the curriculum, but often also a complete pedagogical shift. A good example was COMP 121, in which, by the last revision, individualized learning technique was applied so that each student could not only progress at their own speed, but also choose how deeply they wanted to go into the subject. To entice them to go deeper, a new technology was developed called env3D, that allowed first year students to learn Java programming by writing 3D computer games. The results and feedback from students were amazing.

Cap was, and in some cases still is, the first institution in BC to teach computing science in these innovative ways.

As we know, demand for programs tends to be cyclical, as is the labour market. Since the dot-com bust, the demand for computing scientists has slowly been growing world-wide. Demand for educational programs in computing science has also been growing in response. In fact, the number of students in Computing Science courses started growing again recently, and the department was ready to start rebuilding the second year by offering directed-study courses for students who wanted to stay at Cap to do second-year courses. Although this would have been very economical for the university, the department was never allowed to do so. The short-sighted decision by Cap administration to cut the Computing Science department, at a time when the demand for computing science education is growing, was unfortunate.

All department members very fondly remember the Computing Science departmental meetings. They were more like brainstorming sessions than department meetings. Absolutely everything was shared, successes and occasional failures, and the main imperative was giving the students the best education that could possibly be provided. The faculty left those meetings reenergized. It was a great place to work and the enthusiasm rubbed off on the students, many of them now with established careers in computing science.

The history of the Computing Science department is interwoven in the history of Capilano University. We hope that the cuts of 2013 didn't sever the thread. Hopefully, students at Capilano University will again be offered a 21st century education that includes Computing Science. As our pioneer instructor Peter Palffy showed, when there is a will, there is a way.

INDIVIDUALIZED

JOHN PASS

I BUMPED INTO DERRICK, a former student of mine, in the cavernous Extra Foods mega-mart in Sechelt the other day. "Hey," he said, "a couple of old guys poking around mid-morning in the grocery store."

"Yeah," I replied laconically, "retired. Recreation!" Not quite true. I was loitering with some specific intent, awaiting the filling of a prescription, and I knew from similar encounters in the past that Derrick wasn't retired as I was but on permanent long-term disability with back problems. He'd been an electrician.

If I remember correctly, and there's no guarantee of that given the accumulation of students and years, he'd come to my ABE English course already an electrician in his early thirties, needing writing skills for further specialized training at BCIT, or perhaps because of a promotion at work where he'd be leading a crew, and would need to interpret and explain plans and blueprints, communicate effectively.

I do know that he'd have gone through pretty much the same sequence of assignments in the course that any student of mine did in the 80s. He would have written descriptive, narrative and expository paragraphs, business letters, a resumé, short reports, a research paper. He would have written, unlikely as this sounds today, a book report, though his might have been on a book about dog-breeding, or a computer manual. It had to be a critical assessment, whatever the "book's" subject matter, but a principle of mine was this—*I* want you to do these kinds of writing to learn / demonstrate specific writing skills, but you have to choose the topics being written about. You have to choose the book.

My rationale was that if students chose their own topics it would eliminate one easy cop-out among the many that adults returning to learning (often reluctantly, fearfully) fell back on. They couldn't say, "This doesn't interest me. It's the teacher pushing it. Just like high-school!" And the book report meant they had to go to the Sechelt library, or at least to the laden shelves at the back of the classroom.

In the late 70s and early 80s ABE at Cap was in transition from a well-intentioned but bluntly bureaucratic government program, Basic Training for Skills Development, where course content was simplistic and emphatically laid-out in workbooks, and attendance (especially!) was strenuously policed by the Manpower sponsors.

It didn't work. And we instructors were fortunate to be in an institution that had the flexibility, and trust in our experience and skill, to come up with something that did, a program that wasn't an end in itself but could lead students into further education at Cap or beyond, and / or towards expanded employment options. My strategy with book reports was part of an emerging response at the College to the realization that complex and subtle factors influenced the success of adults returning to learning.

The first thing we did was open up entry. Essentially, anyone could take ABE. We'd accommodate those with learning disabilities or second-language issues or health problems or on parole as best we could alongside the vast majority of applicants who'd dropped out of high school for a myriad of reasons that didn't have much to do with intelligence or ability: to get a job in the once-booming resource economy; to get married; to join a commune or see Mexico.

Secondly, we added flexibility to timetabling and course offerings. Many adult students were taking care of kids, or working part-time. They needed to attend whenever they could in their busy schedules, and extend course-work over more than one term if they could only come to class once or twice a week. To help with motivation we broke the courses themselves into mini-courses so "completion" was more readily attainable, any progress quantified and acknowledged.

We even experimented for a time with *continuous intake,* permitting students to start whenever a course was in session. So the program became *self-paced.* Most importantly, wherever possible, we *individualized* instruction. (Like that term dear to the hearts of faculty, *regularized,* the jargon has always grated, but is efficient in this instance, and historically accurate.)

The course-work was structured and articulated to take individuals where they needed or wanted to go next, but only with their shared commitment. *Choose your own topic.*

Classes that were open to students from a broad range of backgrounds and accomplishment, with a multiplicity of goals and widely different start dates and timetables and rates of progress, were not especially conducive to social bonding, to the shared experience of a cohort. In English I tried to ameliorate that with lots of opportunity for discussion, an instructional element entirely absent from BTSD and most "skills training" curricula at the time.

Everyone had to introduce a discussion topic to the class early, but not too early, in their course. Some factual background information would have to be gathered and imparted, and a statement made of the speaker's position, controversial or not, on the topic or issue. Later a component of the research project assignment entailed presenting that paper to the class or a small group. After a working lifetime of teaching I'm more convinced than ever that discussion at every level, from kindergarten to eldercollege, is a pillar of education and democracy. I'm shocked that it is so often seen as a digression, a waste of time that could be better utilized focused on some ostensibly measurable learning outcome.

At Capilano's "satellite" (later "regional") campuses there were additional challenges for faculty and students. Few students really wanted (or were able without public transit) to navigate dark, wintry coast roads, especially after a day of work or caring for kids. So while the enthusiasm for night classes was continually high, attendance was not good. In the beginning there was little specialized student support on site: sporadic counselling services, no ESL, no library. And even with success, having taken that first step, or a next step, in their adult educational / vocational lives (we stressed this perspective over the notion of a last "finishing high school" step) ABE students on the coast often faced the daunting prospect of having to leave the area (and sometimes partners, kids, familiar jobs, community support) for more education or better work.

ABE was the first program established at the regional campuses, until last year (when it was cut entirely at Squamish) the only consistently available one and, I think it's fair to say, the College's core offering beyond Lynnmour. I thought of the program as the college within the College, working for and embodying Cap's best values: inclusion, comprehensiveness, community and (yes, even at the college prep level!) academic excellence. We were the bedrock.

Some programs that emerged in Sechelt such as Women's Job-Readiness Training and Native Job-Readiness Training, spin-offs of ABE with a devolved focus, were short-lived. Purportedly they were to prepare students rapidly, efficiently, for employment. But what jobs were there for adults with poor work history and numerous health or social issues, who now had from their college experience a résumé, some New Age "*you* can do it" bumpf, and little else? Even low-level entry employment was already filled or going to high school students able to work part-time without benefits. I taught in NJRT and WJRT with initial optimism, but came to see that there are very few simple shortcuts up the ladder.

Education will always remain a mysterious and extraordinarily complex process on an individual and cultural level, but it's also true that most human beings somehow manage to learn what they need to learn when they need to learn it. Any successful educational institution needs to dance with that awkward truism, accommodate unpredictability, cast a wide enough net of opportunity to catch individuals at those idiosyncratic intersections of motivation and necessity. You'll have guessed from what I've written so far that I'm a generalist. Strenuous specialization, or second-guessing of external forces, or rapt devotion to funding efficiencies, reduces an institution's responsiveness to people's and society's real, complex and messy needs.

Everyone who has taught at Cap will have a favourite example of how the College ideally served a student. Mine is the case of Michael, another young man coming into my course in the 80s, coming out of a dying logging industry, without much of a clue about what to do next, and little confidence in his ability.

One of the most interesting lessons for me in teaching adults has been to see how often the best students initially underestimate their abilities, a nasty side-effect of isolated or neglected intelligence and imagination. Michael was curious but cautious, loved to read, wanted to work hard. He expressed an interest in psychology and wrote with much serious effort and revision an excellent research essay on a topic in the field. He was launched: UT (university transfer) program at Cap, BA in Psychology at UNBC, post-grad work.

The last time he dropped by the Sechelt campus, he was in the midst of a speaking tour of US universities, delivering papers at psychology conferences. He's a remarkable exception, certainly. But one that proves the principle of open access, comprehensiveness and flexibility at the far end of the scale, where possibility dwells.

As for the other end of the educational enterprise, mundane reality, most ABE students stay closer to home. It's a small community here on the Sunshine Coast, and I see them all the time. Diana, the successful realtor, is pictured atop pages of properties in the local paper. Another Diana was already a grandmother by the time she became a student of mine in her early forties. At seventeen and pregnant in the 60s she'd lived her first winter on the coast in a teepee at *Babyland*, a commune in Roberts Creek. She was the biggest-hearted and most astonishingly effective co-educator I've ever encountered, encouraging everyone else, loving the interaction, the social dynamics of learning. It might have been she who told me—after a discussion of abortion or gay marriage or someone's idea of a perfect Christmas had taken up way more class time than I'd intended—"We kept talking right through lunch. It's like Oprah!" Last week I spent some time chatting with her at the nursery about raspberry plants to supplement some she gave me decades ago that are still producing.

There are too the sad *non-completions*, whom I and the

program and the College failed despite our best efforts: like Larry, a Carrier-Sekani band councillor, deeply thoughtful and empathetic but unable to write more than a few sentences of poignant story-telling for any assignment; or David, whose disheveled, homeless, schizophrenic ghost I still see around town.

But Rebecca, and Kim, and Tracy became (wow!) writers. I taught the guy who drove the bus for awhile, once we actually got some public transit, but whose real passion is beautifully crafted wooden furniture. And the last time I took the ferry to the North Shore, the self-possessed young Native woman who made my double espresso at the Langdale terminal 'Wheatberries' hut was a former student too.

"How are you doing?" I asked her, trying in vain to recall her name.

"Great, John," she replied. "I just completed a flight attendant course."

"So the next time we meet could be on WestJet!"

"Well, there's a waiting list. . . but one day."

She didn't say my class had helped her get where she was, poised to fly off the coast, and I didn't ask. I wasn't making a survey. But I bet her time as a Cap student fits into her life story in a meaningfully *self-paced* way. Sorry as I was to have forgotten her name, that human moment was a reminder that institutions forget too. And they need to remember, and honour, if not the details at least the broad well-founded principles of the past—education at its best is, as it has long strived to be at Capilano—inclusive, community-based, comprehensive. *Individualized!*

GETTING TO WHERE WE ARE IN COMMUNICATIONS

LESLIE SAVAGE

THE COMMUNICATIONS Department at Capilano was established as a break-away from the English department in the 1970s, long before my time. Crawford Kilian started the department, with a strong belief in writing for practical rather than academic purposes; Crof's original *Communications Book* became almost a training manual for other faculty as the department grew. We functioned as a service department to career programs such as Tourism, Outdoor Recreation, Business, Textiles, Medical Assistant and Legal Assistant, Graphic Arts and Infotec. Communications was an essential course in many programs, with a focus on business writing skills necessary to the program area.

Curriculum planning was often done jointly with the program base areas. This gave Communications faculty, over the years, a broad view of college activities in the career areas as we worked with faculty to innovate materials suitable for students entering different walks of life. Administratively, it gave faculty exposure to the different climates in which various departments operated, as well as to the widely disparate practices when it came to how departments carried on their business. Attending a meeting in the Legal Assistant Department, for instance, was a totally different experience than meeting with the Outdoor Reckies.

The downside of this service-department direction was a large bundle of curriculum development work as faculty tried to please at least twenty different program areas. Interesting work, as it meant learning a lot about the program area, but frustrating too. Thus in the mid-1980s we spoke increasingly in our own department meetings of developing an in-house Communications program. We did develop a five-course certificate program, but the program was simply not strong enough to attract very many candidates.

The beginning of real expansion in the department perhaps began when in January, 2005, I returned after a one-semester leave of absence and found on my voice mail a message from two outsiders, Rick Staehling and Sue Dritmanis. They wanted to meet with me to discuss the possibility of starting a magazine publishing program.

I was intrigued. As a magazine junkie and sometime instructor in a magazine article-writing course, I wondered what it was about Capilano that would attract two successful writer-designers from the publishing industry.

It turned out they had already spoken to Crof at the College about their idea. His response had been, great idea but we don't have the funding to start a program like that, and well, it takes an awfully long time to go through the approval process, and on the whole, probably not a realistic possibility.

All of those things were true. But there were Rick and Sue in my office, and I was impressed by their persistence, by their faith in the idea, and also, I think in hindsight, by what I saw as their potential as Capilano instructors. They had energy and integrity and obviously a strong sense of the potential for a magazine program. These guys had a lot to contribute, and I wanted them in our department.

Sue, Rick and I had several meetings and put together a draft for a program that would be a summer post-graduate boot-campish experience for students wanting to start work in magazines the fall after an internship. With support from Catherine Vertesi, then our dean, and many staff members, we got the program up and running for July and August of 2006, with just over twenty candidates.

Rick and Sue joined the department first in the Magazine Publishing Program, and eventually as faculty teaching other courses in Communications. Sue Dritmanis pursued her master's degree and is now coordinator of the department. The Magazine Publishing Program now registers about 25 students a year, placing graduates in magazines across Canada.

What I learned from the magazine publishing start-up was something that quite startled me: working through the summer was actually a very pleasant experience. Vancouver's temperate climate means summertime on campus is one of the most agreeable times at Capilano. Some services were limited, but the staff and administrators nurtured a rare camaraderie with those faculty members who stayed on campus to teach in what was regularly the off season. Of course, it helped that my colleague Azza Sedky was around to keep me company.

Partly because it was so pleasant on campus during the summer, we used that time to develop Communications' next venture, the two-year Diploma program in conjunction with Simon Fraser University.

Bill Van Luven and I collaborated on the initial meetings with SFU. As we prepared for our first meeting with the university Communications Chair, our apprehension was fairly high: how would SFU react to our proposal that we teach basically the first two years of their degree program in Communications? Would we be seen as trying to poach on their turf? Steal their students?

As so often happens in academic life, we were surprised. The SFU people were delighted, it seems, to approve the transfer courses, suggesting that we simply take their course outlines and move them into Capilano's new Diploma in Communications. The reasons eventually became clear: first, their first- and second-year courses were over-subscribed. Communications was the one area of the humanities in many universities, including SFU, that was expanding as students sought to come to grips with the social realities attendant upon new media. As well, graduate students in the burgeoning communications area needed employment.

Putting together the transfer courses was of course just the first step. Approvals from many committees meant rounds of meetings that I stumbled through, making a lot of mistakes but eventually learning how the process worked. As with the Magazine Publishing Program, we embarked on a round of hiring faculty for the new courses. Meetings ensued with Itidal Sadek, Jillian Feist and Cheryl Helm in the Registrar's Office, and with other admin areas, and for the second summer in a row I was able to enjoy not only the April rhododendrons in flower but the late springtime forsythia, then woodland summer-blooming plants that make the Capilano campus such a delight.

Of course, not everyone was pleased with us. Turf wars arose. The designers argued that the magazine program should belong to them, or at least should have been a joint program—and also wanted to adopt the name Communications for themselves. Sociology claimed that as an academic department they should have housed the new SFU transfer courses—who were these upstart folks from Communications, thinking they could run actual academic, rather than service, courses? All I could do was try to smooth ruffled feathers and hope, possibly in vain, that no hard feelings would endure.

Program development gave me among the most gratifying experiences of my working life—the others being my assignments in Lebanon and China. It is of course satisfying now to see five different programs in Capilano's School of Communications, and know that it was us—Crof, Martin, Azza, me and Bill and Mary Giovanetti—who made this happen, with the support of Catherine Vertesi as dean and then as VP, and later Sue and Ted and Rick and since then others who have joined the department.

When we embarked on our program of expansion to bring Communications to the fore as its own independent program area, we had no idea that a Communications degree, laddered with the certificate and diploma programs, would be the result. In the best Capilano style, developing these programs was at every stage a joint effort by faculty, administration and staff. I thank all the Communications department faculty, the many staff members who supported us, and Catherine and Itidal in administration, for their help in preparing the ground for these programs, then making them fly. We did some good work, and it endures.

THE HISTORY OF THE CAPILANO UNIVERSITY TEXTILE ARTS DEPARTMENT

ANTHEA MALLINSON

THE 40-YEAR-OLD Textile Arts department at Capilano University is grounded in the arts and crafts movement of the 1960s and 70s. Handcraft House, the influential clay and textiles retail store and school on lower Lonsdale in North Vancouver, had nurtured the crafts movement in Vancouver, and was a predecessor of the current well-established Textile Arts Diploma and Advanced Certificate, with degree completion agreements across the country.

When I joined Capilano College in 1988, the Clay and Textiles program was in its made-to-measure weaving and surface design rooms in the Arbutus building. Founder Rose Naumann had just retired and co-founders Leslie Richmond and Mieneke Mees were coordinating and teaching.

All the Arts, at one time, had been together in the Arbutus building. When it was recognized in the 1970s that a number of separate departments needed to be formed, the newly named Studio Arts department moved up to its present location. Clay and Textiles was formed and, along with the Crafts Instructors Training Program, remained in Arbutus.

Under the Clay and Textiles curriculum structure, all first-year students had classes in both subject areas (as well as other support classes to fulfill the diploma). Students selected their chosen focus of either clay or textiles for their second year of studies. In 1992 the small size of the second-year classes created by this structure initiated a comprehensive program review.

Faculty participated fully in the review; the review committee was chaired by then Dean John Waters.

Vancouver's textiles community's unsolicited response to the review was so overwhelmingly supportive of textiles, that Dean Waters recommended the creation of the Textile Arts Department and the two-year Textiles Diploma whose basic structure continues today.

Mieneke Mees, who contributed to this extensive review shortly before her retirement, invited textile artist Ruth Scheuing to apply for the upcoming teaching position. Ruth was hired in 1992.

The names and rough dates of the Textile Arts faculty are as follows:

Rose Naumann 1972–88
Lesley Richmond 1974–98
Mieneke Mees 1975–92
Anthea Mallinson 1988– present
Ruth Scheuing 1992– present
Eleanor Hannan 1996– present
Mary Lou Trinkwon 1997– present
(With visiting artists, master class and short-term faculty including Yvonne Wakabayashi).

Our textiles technicians from 1988 are:

Barbara Cohen
Mary Lou Trinkwon
Trena Coulter
Petyna Bougie

This department has long been touted as one of the unique gems of Capilano College / University and a treasure of the

North Shore. When suspension of the program was suddenly and unexpectedly announced in late April 2013, the community response was sufficiently strong to impress upon the faculty and the community at large that this small department has had a national and international footprint.

The well-connected textiles community has been nourished and influenced by the department, its faculty, current students and accomplished alumni. To quote from Betyna Matzkuhn's 2011 *Surface Design Association Journal*, "The program strives to balance 'creative experimentation, technical process, academic learning, and critical skills,' giving students an impressive toolbox . . . One senses the momentum and potential the program has set off."

One of the educational goals and achievements of the department was to establish block transfer agreements so that students could complete their bachelor's degrees at Emily Carr University of Art and Design, Alberta College of Art, Concordia University and Nova Scotia School of Art and Design.

Ministry statistics demonstrate that students are wholeheartedly satisfied.

The far-reaching breadth and depth of the program use and go well beyond its stated skills-based structure. This is facilitated through the accumulated wealth of knowledge and experience of the committed professional faculty, all of whom work within different aspects of the field of textiles.

It is to be hoped that this accumulated wealth of knowledge and process will be transformed and transferred to a form and location that can continue to explore the field and to nourish the vital and supportive 21st century textile arts community in Vancouver.

THE FRENCH PROGRAMS AT CAPILANO COLLEGE

OLGA KEMPO

I ARRIVED AT CAPILANO COLLEGE on August 1, 1974. My PhD thesis was finally completed in October of that year. Members of the French Department in 1974 included Frank Reid and Joyce Jacquet. We were later joined by Louise Cantin Orr-Ewing in 1976. Guy St. Pierre came from Quebec for one year.

It was to be an exciting time. Bilingualism and Biculturalism were in the air. We were tired of answering the question: Do you teach Parisian French? We wanted to teach a more Canadian-oriented French.

There were great possibilities regarding funding. We received support from the Quebec government for our cultural events thanks to the assistance of the Deputy Minister of Intergovernmental Affairs, Monsieur Robert Normand. The Summer Language Bursary Programs were funded by the Canadian government via the Secretary of State. Louise Krohn took on the task of administering these Summer Language Bursary programs; students were billeted with local families.

Here is a résumé of our activities between 1974–79 at the Institut des Etudes Québécoises:

Academic courses:

Language: Dialogue Canada classes.

Cultural: Quebec Civilization in English and in French.

Literature: Introduction to Quebec Literature.

Community Education Courses: Daytime, evenings, weekends and long distance learning.

Summer programs:
For high school students: Immersion (Langley).
For college and university students: Summer Language Bursary Programs.
For mature students: Travel-Study Exchange Program to Trois-Rivières; this involved two weeks in Trois-Rivières and ran between 1975 and 1980.
For teachers: Upgrading programs (McBride, Lac Le Jeune, North Vancouver).

Conversation classes were led by Marie Bourgeois-Truman, Micheline Pellerin, Jeanette Gacina, Ghislaine Geneau, Lyse Guay, Andrée Marcon, Yolande Morin, Hugette Lacourse, Gabriel Lachance, Elisabeth Peckstadt, and many others over the years.

Especially memorable were the Quebec Profiles, hosted by Laurier Lapierre. They included some of the most remarkable Quebecers of the time, speaking on major issues:

October 1, 1979: Women in Quebec: Hon. Lyse Payette, Minister of Consumer and Corporate Affairs and Financial Institutions in the Quebec Provincial Assembly; a former journalist and broadcaster.
November 5, 1979: Business in Quebec: Pierre Desmarais, Mayor of Outremont and ex-president of Conseil du patronat (Employers' Council)
February 4, 1980: Labour in Quebec: Louis Laberge.
March 3, 1980: Media in Quebec: Evelyn Dumas, Former Editor-in-Chief of Le Jour, Montreal

Continuing after 1979 was a successful Poetry Reading Series funded by the Canada Council; it brought Michèle Lalonde, Michel Tremblay, Roch Carrier, Marie Claire Blais, Yolande Villemaire, Gaston Miron and Nicole Brossard to Vancouver.

In the spring of 1982 we celebrated La Semaine Québecoise with artists Sylvain Lelièvre, Diane Tell, and Arthabaska

In 1991 Lyne Gareau joined the College as a part-time instructor. She was instrumental in creating the Language Lab and Resource Centre, situated in the Arbutus Building. She spent five years consulting with various departments to make it the success that it is today.

I retired in 1998 after 24 exciting, exhilarating, challenging years at Capilano College. I think we succeeded in bringing British Columbia and Quebec closer together. French as spoken in Canada was now the norm.

the **informer**

Volume VII No. 1 January 14, 1985

North Cafe gets new chef

Beaver Foods in the North Cafeteria is proud to welcome a new chef. Joe Raschendorfer is a chef with 33 years of experience in hotel and institutional cooking. He started his apprenticeship in Germany in 1952 and comes to us from another Beaver operation. Joe would like to invite everyone to experience his culinary talents at a "Break the Ice" buffet to be held on January 24.

Are you into cameras?

If you have been thinking about taking a Media Resources course, think fast. If you hurry there may still be some spots left in Media 070 - Basic Photography, Media 074 - Basic Film-Making, Media 082 - Micro computer Graphics, or Media 090 - Independent Production. For more details contact the department.

15 students will head for Quebec

Meet Cap's Quebec Exchange students. These 15 lucky people will be going to Ahuntsic College in Montreal at the end of April, and in the meantime they have been hosting the Ahuntsic students who arrived here on January 4. Our students are: (First row) Margaret Crowley, N.Van., Karla Campbell, W.Van., Dr. Olga Kempo, Instructor, Sally McDermott, W.Van., Christine Nordstrom, N.Van., Mary Ann McLuckie, W.Van. (Back row) Irwin Oostindie, N.Van., Bruce Wallace, N.Van., Pat Von Blumen, N.Van, Dougie Fraser, N.Van., and Sheila Smail, N.Van. Missing from photo are David Dungey, N.Van, Kathy Newman, N.Van, Debbie Parliament, Burnaby, and Todd Wong, N.Van.

capilano college

DEVELOPMENT OF THE FIRST HEALTH SERVICES AT CAPILANO COLLEGE

CATHERINE ZUEST

IN THE 1970S, I was a Registered Nurse attached to the North Shore Health Service working as a Community Health Nurse. My position was seconded to Capilano College in the mid-1970s. With that, I was assigned the task of establishing a health care service for the College. To that point, all that had been available was a first aid station. The focus of my work was on prevention.

At the start, there was no working space available on the campus. I shared part of a trailer with Neil Chester, the Physical Education coordinator. Construction was completed of the ND building on the North Campus, and this became the future site of Health Services.

In my new capacity, I attended support staff meetings and started determining the health needs of students and staff. I was also able to collaborate with contacts in other colleges and the University of British Columbia in an endeavour to set up a basic structure. That early operation became the foundation of Capilano College's Health Service.

It was nothing grand! The North Campus ND building space was very small—enough to accommodate my office, supplies, a waiting area and a day cot. Once the sign was on the door, students and staff began to drop by with their health concerns. I dealt with a range of health-related issues including questions and concerns about nutrition, family planning, lifestyle changes, fitness and emotional and stress-related problems.

Through my connections at the University of British Columbia, I was approached and asked to become involved in a lifestyle survey being conducted by the federal and provincial governments. The goal of this research was to determine the general health and needs of Capilano College students.

Around that time, psychologist Dr. Alan Best at University of British Columbia had developed and was offering a smoking cessation course. Again, I was asked to facilitate that program at Capilano College, as well as a stress management course. I set up small smoking cessation groups, held in the evenings, for students, faculty and staff. The results compared very favourably with the research groups of Dr. Alan Best. I continued to offer courses in stress management both one to one and in small groups.

Health Services also offered counselling, as requested, by individuals or groups. Education sessions on health concerns or sex education were also offered.

First aid was included. There was a first aid station set up in space on South Campus. It was managed, as needed, by a staff member with first aid training.

Since I was required to develop a budget for capital and operating costs, I sought and received assistance from some of the faculty members. In time, it became necessary to have an assistant. The College then hired another Registered Nurse to assist with provision of health services. After that, a physician was hired to be on campus one or two days a week.

After about five years, I returned to my work as a Community Health Nurse with the North Shore Health Department. I left with fond memories of having developed an integrated health service uniquely tailored to the needs of post-secondary and mature students, with the ultimate support and co-operation of the faculty and staff.

MY EDUCATION AS A TEACHER AT CAPILANO COLLEGE

BOB SHERRIN

I CAME TO CAPILANO COLLEGE in the early 1980s. My only previous post-secondary teaching consisted of a summer course and one fall course, both in Creative Writing, at UBC. There, I worked solo, no department members to advise me or ease classroom jitters, no tales, no lessons learned

Some time later, I was lucky enough to publish a short story in *The Capilano Review*. Its editor, Bill Schermbrucker, invited me to read to one of his Creative Writing classes. I was drawn to the energy in that room, the open discussion, the frankness, the fun. At the end of the class, Bill challenged his students to write a new piece for next week's meeting, then turned to me and said, "That includes you, too, if you're willing." I wrote a short story during the next seven days, and returned to Bill's class—again the intensity of listening and talking.

That first taste of Capilano College pleased and intrigued me. Through Bill, I met a few members of the English department. Good conversations, from pedagogy to plain talk. They were the English department. When colleagues from other areas dropped by, I saw that all of them were Capilano College.

Yes, we worked in conventional disciplines under written codes of conduct and contracts of employment. However, I was surprised as a teacher new to Cap, that I designed my own courses and selected my own curriculum, changed it, bettered it, changed it again. I wasn't given a template, other than the restrictions of course outlines. I team-taught, crossed discipline borders, played myself in a student production. Steadily found my place.

The CCFA helped build Capilano College. As a temp (a non-regular instructor) for ten years, I attended meetings, negotiation reports, strike votes, and walked picket lines. I and other Non Regs won the right to proper benefits. CCFA members pushed for a campus where administration and faculty worked through problems together: consulted, debated, disagreed, yet achieved a collegiality that required much more than professional politeness.

My colleagues taught me to teach, taught me to follow my instincts as a writer and educator, gave me resources and expertise, consolation. How did we teach? Daily. In classrooms, hallways, cafeterias, on the walk from North to South, wherever students and teachers found themselves together. That's how we taught, that's how I learned.

My education as teacher grew even more when I began to go to Cap College's satellites, campuses located in Sechelt and Squamish, plus Mount Currie, home of the Lil'wat First Nation.

The Sechelt campus consisted of a single building, part of which, I believe, had once served as mechanics' training site. Diane Staples was our DDA; in other words, the campus didn't function without Diane's constant work and creativity.

The seasonal pleasures of Sechelt are many, but my students were weekly pleasures. They represented a cross-section of the coastal community: forest-workers who'd lost their jobs when that sector declined, now seeking an education that would help them build a new work life; an RCMP constable, completing required courses, who did his research on marijuana grow-ops on the coast; the many members of the Sechelt First Nation who wanted to continue their educations, including the chief. The

Sechelt people collectively taught me the power and necessity of storytelling.

When I was working in Sechelt, BC Ferries cut the 10 p.m. sailing to Horseshoe Bay, and I had no way home after class ended at 9:30. I asked my dean for accommodation. I was told that wasn't possible. In reply, I said, "So, the College will take care of my car (legitimate travel expense) but not me." For the rest of that term, I slept on a couch in the College's lounge, said goodnight to the cleaners who came through, and rose at 5:30 am to eat the container of granola and milk I'd brought with me. Then I took the first ferry back to the mainland and taught more classes.

Squamish was a similarly small campus with classes of dedicated students from all walks of life: pipefitters, fishers, retirees, high school students, and the wife of a local RCMP officer. They all wanted to learn, which made teaching easy and very rewarding.

Our weekly custom was to finish class, have a beer together at The Chieftain, talk about our lives and hopes. Then I drank coffee and hit the Squamish Highway back to my tiny apartment in Vancouver. On one such drive, I came across a very nervous young man whose car had slid off the road and was hung-up near the edge of a precipice. He clearly needed help and clearly didn't want the RCMP involved. Because he was also driving a Volkswagen squareback like mine, I knew it performed in ways unlike that of other cars. I got behind the wheel, trusted in the rear-engine weight of the VW, put it into first gear, and slowly pulled the car forward enough that my nervous companion could take over.

Mount Currie was a revelation to me. A stunningly beautiful area, it is the traditional, unceded territory of the Lil'wat people, and I was there to teach a class of women who needed English 100 to complete their NITEP (Native Indian Teachers Education Program) credentials.

We met in a one-room schoolhouse. I soon learned how much these women had to teach me, most often during our tea breaks: their determination to revive their village and others through education; to fight against the alcoholism that had taken so many of their men. One student happily told me that she wouldn't be in class next week because her family was celebrating the first anniversary of her husband's sobriety.

These women told me about residential schools and the horrors experienced there. One quietly explained that she was forced to wash her face in a solution of water and bleach to lighten her skin colour.

Eventually, some of my students began to bring their children to class, so they could improve their English, though one of them told me he was most happy that elders were now coming to their day-school to teach the Lil'wat language.

Later, it was the women of Mount Currie who occupied the offices of the Department of Indian Affairs to protest the sexism embedded in the Indian Act that forced First Nations women to give up native status if they married a white man, while the white wife of a native man gained status.

I have no doubt that the women of Mount Currie taught me far more than I taught them. Cap's relationship with the people of Mount Currie has now grown to the point where courses are regularly offered there, no longer in the old schoolhouse, but in a small complex of buildings dedicated to the education of native people. I like to think that some of my former students brought about that transformation. They most certainly had the power and determination to do it.

In truth, I believe my most important and gratifying work as a teacher took place in Sechelt, Squamish, and Mount Currie. There I saw weekly how a community could grow and restore itself when Capilano College reached deeply into the communities it served.

I may have referred to those campuses as "satellites," but they were absolutely central to the institution's goals. There, I most deeply experienced the power of Capilano College to help people restore their lives, their hope for future growth of their communities, and the means to achieve it.

WHY OUR STUDENTS REMEMBER US

PENNY LECOUTEUR

As I was sitting in a local coffee shop last week, chatting and enjoying a latte with a friend, a middle-aged man came over. "Hello, Penny. Good to see you, and you haven't changed a bit." (Not true but it was nice of him to pretend.) "And you still sound the same." (That bit is probably true.) It was, of course, one of my ex-students.

I didn't really remember him. As I said, he was a middle-aged man and he had changed quite a bit since he was a seventeen- or eighteen-year-old in one of my classes at Capilano College. But there was something vaguely familiar about him and when he told me his name I could—again vaguely—remember that. We chatted for a few minutes: The "what are you up to now" and the "I retired a few years ago" routine, and then he went on his way. My friend smiled at me. She has seen this happen many times over the years and was used to listening in on these mini-reunions.

But it got me to thinking. There have been quite a number of students in my classes that by any normal measure in our society, have been great successes. Some became doctors, others dentists or veterinarians. There are the lawyers, the professors and the researchers, politicians, entrepreneurs, CEOs and many other important and worthwhile achievers. These are the ones we celebrate at alumni dinners, honour with awards and citations, and whose accomplishments we describe for the press.

And then there are the many more who are all achievers in their own way. They are the ones who have become capable and useful citizens without having their feats and triumphs recognized in public. And I am just as proud of these ex-students as I am of the first group. Some of my ex-students still keep in touch even after decades; I have gone to weddings and PhD defences, I get Christmas cards and new baby announcements, we meet for coffee when they are in town and I even visit a few when I go out of town. I may have had an effect on their lives, but they have also had an effect on mine.

I went for a flu shot a few years ago. The nurse doing the jabbing started the conversation off by asking if I remembered her. Evidently she still attributes her success at getting into nursing school to my CHEM 030 class. Her oldest daughter was in high school, and she was proud that she remembered enough chemistry to be able to explain some of the concepts the daughter had encountered in grade eleven chemistry.

After retiring, I started to play badminton with a group who have been playing together for a number of years. I was visiting at one of their homes recently and her daughter arrived. She gaped at me. "Mum, this is Penny – the organic chem prof from Cap. The one I was always telling you about." My new friend was dumbfounded. "I never put the pieces together." And then her son-in-law appeared; he'd been in the organic chem class too.

Some of these encounters can be funny. There was the summer morning just before 8:00 a.m. when I was sipping my coffee, still wearing my pajamas. Suddenly I heard that ominous rumbling. "The garbage!" I yelled, flying outside to gather up the garbage can and push it down to the bottom of the drive just as the district's garbage truck pulled up. As I flew back up the driveway (I was in my pj's, after all) I heard one of the garbage collectors call out, "Hello, Penny. See where my chemistry got me?"

And then there was the time when my mother was staying with us and we went to a BC Liquor Store for a bottle of wine. "Hello, Penny," said the young man at the checkout counter. "Nice to see you again."

"He was one of my students a few years ago," I told my mother. A week or so later we went into another BC Liquor Store and the same thing happened with a different young man at the counter. After the third time this happened, at a third liquor store, my mother was firmly convinced that the "he was in my chem class" explanation was suspect.

But the stories can also be quite sobering. One student came up to the College to see me in my office. It was a number of years since he had been in my class, and I knew that he had been in jail on drug-dealing charges.

"I was stupid," he told me. "I got in with the wrong crowd and thought this was how to make money." He said that while he was in jail he kept thinking of something that I had said to him as I handed back his mid-term exam. I couldn't remember anything special that I had said, but evidently his mid-term mark was good, much better than the previous semesters where his performance was average, and I had said something like "I always knew you were capable of doing well."

He had sat in jail mulling over his future and kept thinking that Penny had thought he had ability; that thought kept him going. He subsequently returned to university, finished his degree, was now married and employed. He had turned his life around and he wanted to tell me that it was my off- the-cuff remark that had kept him going.

Another time, a mature ex-student came by my office to see me. Her family had been having a particularly difficult time. Her kids were sick a lot, especially her son: headaches, nausea, and listlessness. He had missed a lot of school and didn't seem to be getting any better. She suddenly remembered something that I had said in a chemistry class—that carbon monoxide poisoning is difficult to detect because its symptoms are flu-like. Her son had just tested positive for carbon monoxide poisoning; his bedroom was in the basement right next to the furnace, which was now shown to be emitting this odorless, toxic gas. She wanted to let me know and thank me. Don't believe that something you say can't have a life-changing outcome!

I've sat in a chair in a dental specialist's office while the two hygienists from the next office came in to see me. They'd seen my name on the patient list and wanted to meet their "old chem prof" again. Great reunion despite the fact that my jaw and lips were so numb I could hardly talk. Even my own doctor obliged; the young locum she had hired for a four-week vacation had been one of my students.

My kids got in on the action too. They complained that everywhere they went with me, I ran into ex-students. Once, my then fourteen-year-old son grumbled that the guy in the bike shop had spent more time talking to me than helping him with the all-important mountain-bike selection process. "What's your problem?" I asked him. "He gave you 15% off because he took my chemistry course five years ago."

I have had an e-mail from an ex-student I hadn't heard from for at least ten years. She is now a chemistry professor at a big university in the US and she just wanted me to know that whenever she lectured about one particular topic, she would always hear my voice in her head explaining the theory.

For these students, and many, many more, Capilano College

was special. The class size was small—well, smallish. Small enough, anyway, to allow you to know your prof, to ask questions in class and get the answers right away, to feel comfortable discussing issues and sharing opinions. And when you left and went on to one of the big "real" universities, it was still to Cap that you would return to see your prof and ask if they would write you a reference for grad school or med school or whatever. Because no one at their present university (i.e., their professors) knew who they were, and they felt comfortable coming back to Cap where they knew and were known.

Looking back on all the great memories that I have of being part of Cap, I think the most treasured are of the students who were in my classes. If my experience with ex-students is typical (and I'm pretty sure it is), then what a huge effect Capilano College and now Capilano University has had and is having on kids from all over the North Shore and beyond.

Multiply my approximately two hundred and fifty students a year by the number of years I was in the classroom, and it comes to over eight thousand. Multiply this by the number of faculty over these years, and we are talking hundreds of thousands. And it all started with a few late afternoon and evening classes in West Vancouver Secondary in 1968.

WRITING CENTRE / WRITING ACROSS THE CURRICULUM

ROSEMARY COUPE

THE CONCEPT OF A Writing Centre—a free service open to all College students and aiming to foster excellence in their writing—was relatively new to BC when the Capilano College Writing Centre had its modest beginning in 1985. It started in the space now on the south side of the Library building, then known as the "B" building and the original home of the Humanities Division at Lynnmour. By the mid-80s, however, it was occupied by the Achievement Resource Centre. ARC Coordinator Ruth D'Hollander and Divisional Assistant Lynn Hamilton were very cooperative in their attitude towards the Writing Centre and its students, allocating an office for our use. Students signed up for half-hour appointments on the door outside the office.

From the beginning, though, the Centre was an English department initiative, funded by English department sections, and owing much to the energy of Jean Clifford, one of the English coordinators at the time. Jean was also one of the three department faculty assigned to the Centre, and she designed a grand scheme for Writing Centre handouts covering all aspects of academic writing. Over the first couple of years we wrote the handouts, and their descendants (still numbered according to Jean's system) are in the Writing Centre today.

Student demand for the Writing Centre was strong from the beginning. After the first couple of years, Jean Clifford (still English coordinator) persuaded Dean Bill Gibson that the Centre should move closer to the English department. Bill originally wished to keep ARC, the Writing Centre, and the Math Learning Centre together as services for all students. However, we felt that the function of ARC was remedial, and we did not want the Centre to be primarily remedial. We also felt that the English department would take ownership of the Centre if it was attached to their physical space, and students too would associate the Centre with our department and understand the full range of services we offered.

So we moved to our first temporary home in Humanities, the small open area and three offices at the north end of the Humanities office corridor. This was still quite cramped, but it did allow us to set up computers for student use in the corner office. When the computers arrived, we had to learn to use them ourselves. Reid Gilbert gave Penny Connell and me a crash course, his fingers flying over the keys. Occasionally computers themselves crashed and essays were swallowed. We were lucky that the computer support people were generous with their time.

Establishing the Centre as a drop-in service made much better use of instructor time and also increased student demand, so in fall 1989 we moved into a larger space, what had been the lounge area to the right of the Humanities entrance. This meant that several faculty were displaced from the adjacent three offices. The larger space meant that we were able to build a Writing Centre book collection, consisting of dictionaries, other reference books, and also publishers' free copies of textbooks, kindly donated by English faculty. Students were now able to do their writing in the Centre, often using the computers, and consulting an instructor when necessary. This fitted our emphasis on writing as a process.

We used a tutorial method, encouraging students to talk through their ideas before planning and writing their essays;

often we saw the same student at different stages of work on a major assignment. We recorded the purpose of each student visit, and while the commonest reason for visits in fall 1990 was help with documentation, almost as common was help with organization, outlining, and thesis development—the vitally important thinking skills which underlie writing. We did also offer remedial help: when students brought in a graded assignment (often by referral from their instructor), we went over it with them and tutored them intensively on specific writing skills.

With the move to a larger space, more English sections were dedicated to the Centre. The ESL, Communications, and ABE departments also supported us by funding time for their faculty in the Centre. This enabled us to offer specialized help, to ESL students for example. By the fall of 1989 the Centre was open from 10:30 to 4:30 from Monday to Thursday and also Friday morning. At this time also the English coordinators argued successfully that the Centre needed a convenor with a .5 section time release per semester to do time-tabling, build the handout collection, build and catalogue the book collection, compose publicity materials, write reports, and conduct outreach activities among faculty. I became the first convenor, and was later succeeded by Rae Nickolichuk, Jenny Penberthy, and others.

Student demand for the services of the Centre kept growing. In 1990–91, we had 2,308 visits from students representing 26 disciplines. So in 1992 we argued for a further move, and worked with the dean to find a suitable space. Eventually we fixed on the Faculty-Staff Lounge at the southwest corner of the Fir building, a generous and well-lit space. Again this meant inconvenience to the people who used the lounge, but such was the support for the Centre as a service for all College students that the CCFA and

Staff Association agreed to the move. In 1992–93 we had 3,037 visits. In January 1994 our open hours were extended to Monday through Thursday 8:30 to 5:30.

Students generally understood our policies. They realized that our help would not guarantee them a good grade but would enable them to develop their own ability to write well, and also teach them techniques for planning, writing, editing, and proofreading. We expected them to discover the ideas (helped by questioning designed to draw out the student) and apply the techniques. I remember only one day when a student tried to drop off a rough draft, telling us he'd be back later in the day to pick up the finished product.

Starting in 1989, the Writing Centre was able to reach out into the College community much more as a result of the Writing Across the Curriculum project. The WAC movement, already well established in the US by the middle 1980s, had its primary focus on writing as a tool for learning, not just a test. This meant that written assignments were designed to help students understand course material. Also, instructors responded to student writing in draft form, on the assumption that the whole process of planning, writing and revising leads to learning. Beyond this, the movement emphasized the importance of the specialized language of an academic discipline and, more generally, on writing as an essential skill in life and work.

In 1988 Ruth D'Hollander of the Achievement Resource Centre obtained Ministry funding for her report Meeting New Challenges Across the Curriculum: A Report on Teaching Reading, Critical Thinking and Writing in All Subject Areas. Its chapter on WAC, which I wrote, alludes to the benefits of WAC to students, in helping them learn more effectively, and also to institutions, in bridging gaps between departments and disciplines.

The effect on student learning is of course hard to measure, but the WAC program as it developed at Capilano certainly led to much cross-disciplinary discussion and collegial work among faculty. One of the recommendations of Ruth's report was that the Ministry should fund institutional projects aimed to improve the teaching of reading, critical thinking, and writing skills across the curriculum, and in fact that happened at Capilano.

Having Reid Gilbert as both English department coordinator and Faculty Development Chair in 1988–89 helped push the idea of WAC ahead, linked with a stronger role for the Writing Centre. With support from Deans Bill Gibson and Frank Gelin, Reid obtained release time for Penny Connell and Rosemary Coupe to organize a four-day series of seminars sponsored by the CCFA in May 1989. Attending a meeting at a College Composition and Communication Conference in Seattle put us in touch with leaders of the WAC movement in Washington State, some of whom accepted our invitation to present sessions in May.

An introductory WAC noon session on 31 January 1989 was attended by 40 faculty from across the College, and the May seminars themselves were attended by over 70 faculty. We learned about ways to integrate writing in our courses, including the design of short sequenced assignments relating to course goals. We also addressed practical concerns, like asking students to write more while avoiding an impossible marking load for the instructor. Enthusiasm was high, an advisory group was formed, and several follow-up faculty seminars took place, as well as a one-day workshop offered as part of the CCFA May 1990 program.

Critical factors in the success of our WAC project were the interest from faculty—our Faculty Advisory Group made collective decisions about the directions we took—and the support of administrators. Further release time was given to me in fall 1989 for initiatives based on the Writing Centre. A series of lunch-hour "mini-lectures" ran for several semesters, and some students actually did give up their lunch hours to come. We also offered custom-designed "mini-lectures" in classes across the College, including Biology, Anthropology, and Psychology.

The Faculty Advisory Group agreed on several things: the development of a set of standardized correction symbols for marking essays (in the end, this was not universally accepted); a policy on expectations for student writing published in the Calendar; and greater standardization in documentation systems (with either the current MLA or current APA system, depending on the discipline, replacing the wide range of conventions previously required).

More substantive was the development of the College's own short writing manual, *The Capilano Guide to Writing Assignments.* Largely thanks to the advocacy role played by Humanities Division Chair Penny Connell, Faculty Development Chair Reid Gilbert, and Deans Frank Gelin and John Waters, we obtained a $14,400 grant from the Centre for Curriculum Development that enabled us to offer release time to faculty to act as consultants for the booklet. Towser Jones represented Social Sciences, Vicky Troup Pure and Applied Sciences, and Jessie Pendygrasse Business Management. We met at one another's houses and saw the booklet through various drafts.

The Capilano Guide was first published in 1992. It had three major sections, one describing the writing process, another covering commonly assigned forms of writing in different disciplines, and the third giving detailed information about the MLA and APA systems of documentation. The booklet was sold for under $3 through the College bookstore, and many instructors required their students to have a copy. The rapid development of the internet in particular meant that the *Guide* needed to be updated each subsequent year.

The Writing Across the Curriculum project had one interesting result in terms of curriculum development: the pairing of English 100 composition courses with courses in other disciplines, with the assignments in the English course growing out of the material studied in the other course. This implemented the concept of writing to learn, and was based on the premise that students learn to write best when dealing with subject-matter that interests them. All students in the designated sections registered for both courses, which were scheduled back-to-back to allow for some team-teaching.

A number of faculty gave their time and energy to designing and teaching the paired courses, beginning in Fall 1991. We had English 100 paired with courses in Music, Economics, Sociology, Philosophy, Geography, History, Theatre, and Psychology. The instructors received a modest amount of release time, .25 section per section taught, with the first two pairs funded by our $14,400 grant and a further five pairs funded by a $21,400 grant received a year later.

The more students cared about the subject-matter, the more they seemed to gain from the paired courses and the more they appreciated the solid core which the content course gave to English 100. The instructor of the Music History course wrote, "In the past relatively few of our students stayed in English courses. This year the majority of the students finished English 100 . . . . I found that not only was the writing better but the students knew how to handle research. The vitality of the papers was due I think to the combination of being asked to write about subjects of vital interest to the students along with an acquired ability to express themselves."

The paired courses did create some headaches for administrators. Initially, class size in the non-English course (normally 35) was lowered to the English 100 maximum of 25, since it was essential to have the same group of students in both courses for integration of course outlines and assignments. This occurred at the cost of FTEs, of course. Various inventive solutions to the class size issue were found by Dean John Waters from one semester to the next (for example, setting aside .5 section to fund reductions in class size), but there was no permanent solution.

Other administrative problems occurred when students who did not need to take English 100 wanted to enroll in the content course, or when students found that they had to drop both courses or neither. Students who stayed in the courses, though, found that not only did they offer enriched learning, but the advantage of gaining credit for two courses in which a major assignment, the research essay, often counted for both.

To quote from the Summary of the "Writing Across the Curriculum" chapter in Ruth D'Hollander's report, "Successful WAC programs appear to be based both on faculty enthusiasm and administrative support.... Administrative support must take the tangible form of release time and guarantees of reasonable class size .... " Certainly at Capilano in the late 80s and early 90s we had both those elements. Over the long term, however, mounting budgetary constraints made it impossible for administrators to give guarantees of class size lower than the norm for the discipline. The paired courses continued, but in diminished numbers.

From the beginning, the response of Capilano College instructors to the WAC project showed their willingness to alter established methods of teaching and experiment with new ones in the interests of student learning. The paired courses, in particular, demanded that instructors invest a great deal more time in planning and delivering the courses than normal, as they integrated writing into their courses in new ways. Without the background support of the Writing Centre and the many English, ESL, ABE, and Communications instructors who worked there, as well as the support of administrators, such innovation would not have been possible.

RECOLLECTIONS OF AN OUTDOOR RECKY LIFE

BRIAN WHITE

IN 1971, I'D DECIDED that a life of work in the forest industry wasn't really for me. I didn't have the beer capacity of my fellow workers and always had to shave off my beard and cut my hair before I started work. I had been teaching a couple of sections in geography while finishing my MA at SFU, and Harold Kirchner, the Dean of Careers, asked if I would be interested in starting up an Outdoor Recreation program. We ran a trial project in 1971 in the new Lynn Valley Ecology Centre, and it seemed to go well (at least that's what I said).

So in 1972, we got under way—using the basement of a church in Capilano Village. Looking back, I must admit that the operation was a bit chaotic. I was only a bit older—and in some cases younger—than the students. There might have been an issue with authority in the early days, and with different faculty perspectives on the role of statistics, science education, etc. in the program. At least the students improved their literacy level, under the guidance of Crawford Kilian, and their geographic understanding, with Karen Ewing in charge. Alf Waterman made stats actually enjoyable, and Nancy Ricker taught environmental sciences while Neil Chester taught fitness.

In 1974 we moved onto the Lynnmour campus and developed a successful outdoor expedition program, using the Cathedral Lakes Park and Outward Bound as a leadership training residency. We also hiked some distance into the Pasayten Wilderness in the

USA, and wandered around in there for several trips until the US Forest Service launched a posse in 1976 to arrest us for illegally crossing the border. Blissfully unaware of the fuss we'd created, we were back in Canadian territory before they caught up with us.

Don Basham and Jim Boyd joined us and started up the Wilderness Leadership Program, which was perfectly aligned with the major interest in outdoor activities which characterized the baby boomers of the time. John Hatchard and Tynke Braaksma taught canoeing, taking over from Brian Creer.

In the first year at Lynnmour, Keith Wade and I purchased on behalf of the College a really excellent collection of plants, many of which continue to grace the campus. We moved the focus of the program from more of an environmental education program towards management, to get a better job placement rate, and developed what was to become a successful practicum.

In the late 1970s, we developed the Fitness Leadership program with Andre Vidya-Janyk, training people to be fitness instructors, and also some other programs that were far ahead of their time. These included Leisure Counselling, with Lana-Lee Schmidt leading, and High Adventure Outdoor Pursuits with Roger Griffiths in charge. In 1978, we climbed Mt Waddington for the tenth anniversary of Capilano College. By 1980, we were really on a roll! In that year we started the Horticulture program, which grew quickly into another program appealing to the boomers.

These new programs were starting to make headway when the 1981 recession hit. Leisure Counselling and High Adventure were gone, and we took a real hit in sections. It was after the announcement that BC had secured Expo 86 that we started to think about developing tourism, since the economy—and the demographics—were changing quickly.

In 1985, we introduced a tourism supervisory program at Whistler, and also wrote the Whistler Spirit Program (still there today). Tourism in the mid-late 1980s was hot, so we were able to develop a program at Whistler and then bring it back to the Lynnmour campus and build a Tourism Management Diploma program, which evolved into the tourism degree in the mid-1990s. In the 1990s we also went overseas, a tradition that continues to this day. We started in Thailand, and progressed to Malaysia, Vietnam, and Paraguay.

2014 marks 44 years since I started my own journey in outdoor recreation and tourism. This very incomplete overview will have to do for now. I don't regret a day of it, and I'm still working and hiking and mountain biking. When I actually do retire, I'll get all the memories organized into a proper archive!

TEAM-TEACHING AT CAPILANO COLLEGE

PENELOPE CONNELL

TEAM-TEACHING IS A great example of the excellence Cap so often boasts of. I had my first experience of team-teaching with Bob Gallagher, who taught in the Religious Studies Department in the 1970s. Bob and I taught Comparative Religion and Canadian Literature—an overflow class, overflowing both in interested students and in great material. To this day I recall the heated discussions over the ending of Atwood's *Surfacing.* And Pierre Coupey and I taught Creative Writing in the late 1970s—a life-changing experience for me as a teacher.

From a major conference in Seattle in the early 80s, Rosemary Coupe and I brought big ideas for a conference of Cap's own: Writing Across the Curriculum. She, along with faculty from Humanities, Social and Pure and Applied Sciences and Business, initiated a series of classes, in which instructors from two different disciplines teamed up in the classroom to walk the walk on how writing facilitates learning.

Well over a dozen faculty were involved. I learned all I know about economics by team-teaching with Nigel Amon for a couple of years. Bob Sherrin and I alternated leading our English lit classes, while the other would throw difficult questions from the sidelines. Our students really opened up when they were disabused of the notion of "right answers." Even marking papers with Bob was fun.

I shared my team-teaching career most joyfully with Dawn Moore in the Theatre Department. We offered English 100 /

Theatre History for probably seven or eight years. Here the disagreements were real. With our current qualifications and up-to-the-minute reading on subjects ranging from a re-evaluation of the place of women in Greek society to Peter Brook's use of stage props, we made classes that produced for us big-time. Students made accurate scale models of historic theatres, took the roles of characters in the plays we read, and illustrated dialectical theatre—and did some pretty fine writing!

Team-teaching was a roaring success when one semester Dawn took ill and I found myself in the classroom on my own for a stretch. How I missed her warmth and energy, the way our students laughed when one of us forgot something and the other interjected. They were totally engaged and actively challenged, throwing ideas around in our classes. WAC pedagogy created the ideal teaching situation—depth, serious thought and intellectual stretch all round.

Bob, Bob, Pierre, Nigel, and especially Dawn and I worked at what always felt like the cutting edge, where I got to give more as a teacher than I ever could have on my own, and use what I was learning to advantage in all my classes.

MEMORIES OF CAPILANO

GREG LEE

Bill Schermbrucker asked me to make a contribution to the Cap History book. It is not an easy task. What do I say about what was my working life at one institution for almost 39 years—a working life during which I was a faculty member, a coordinator, a division chair, a registrar, a systems analyst, a dean, a vice-president and president? There are too many memories, but there are a few questions I asked myself.

- How did I get there?
- Why did I stay so long?
- What do I remember best?

How did I get there?

The year is 1971, W.A.C. Bennett is premier and I have essentially completed my thesis. I have been living off what grad students of the day called "a blonde fellowship"—but mine is actually a brunette fellowship. Employment prospects are slim. A new creation—a community college—has opened on the North Shore and is advertising for instructors. Now, I have lived on the North Shore, excluding a brief interlude while I attended UBC, since 1948. (I still do, and that makes 66 years—do the math.) So crossing the Lions Gate Bridge is not at all daunting. Why not apply? I can stay a term or two while my thesis makes it through the formal processes. I'll be gone in a short time.

A short time turned into a lifetime. This story is familiar to many people who worked at Cap.

For me, and for many others, Capilano is a place that keeps

you involved, keeps you contributing and usually keeps you sane. People don't want to leave—and I was captivated like the rest. It is actually a bit magical, but it also probably reflects the fact that we set ourselves up so that everyone is important, and there is relatively little hierarchy.

It may be a small point, but Cap has never had designated parking for anyone—designated spaces, or lots, but no one has had their name on a space unless they won it through the United Way. I remember the very early discussions about washrooms—it seems silly in retrospect but the issue was whether there would be faculty and staff washrooms to keep us separated from the students. Little things do make a difference when you set up an institution.

Maybe it's because we all worked under less than ideal conditions. I recall listening to the 1972 Canada-Russia hockey series over a communal radio that was operated out of the student services / registration area—we could all hear it because we were all in one portable with only cubicles and no real walls or doors. There are still faculty offices not much better.

There was always challenge and a sense that we could and would do more. And we did. There was a sense that we could try something new and, funding issues aside, we were encouraged to do so. It is not an accident that *The Capilano Review*, for example, was started here and not at another college, or that Capilano was the home for *The Westcoast Reader*. There is not another institution that I know of that can claim such a wide diversity of highly recognized publications.

And then there was the move to Lynnmour. Despite the sparse buildings, it was clear the campus would eventually be very special. What happened was that I got caught by the Cap recruitment and retention strategy: Encourage participation and creativity in a beautiful setting.

Fast forward 38 years, 10 premiers, three children and four grandchildren.

Why did I stay so long?

I estimate I drove about 100,000 miles between my home near Edgemont Village and Lynnmour over 37 years. A long way, six different vehicles, but never feeling like I didn't want to go to work—except perhaps during the labour disputes in the very early days!

One of the real perks of working at Capilano is that you are constantly surrounded by young people, and as I said before, we are not segregated. We never had luxurious executive offices—not even a board room. There is no faculty club or executive dining room. Surrounded by youth, I didn't view myself as the old white-haired guy at the coffee stand—even though I eventually was. There are good reasons not to have mirrors around.

So, time just flew by because of the good fortune I had to be part of Capilano and the youth that are the very reason for its existence.

What do I remember best?

I remember 38.5 years at the same institution, and the privilege of being one of its presidents. The highest praise I have ever received was when, after 23 years working at Capilano, mostly in administration, hence "on the dark side," and despite therefore everyone knowing all my flaws and foibles probably better than I knew them myself, I was asked to be president. It remains my biggest vote of confidence.

I remember continuing to "bask in the reflected glory of the many accomplished people at Capilano."

I remember enjoying my role to do what I could to get the creative energies of the institution all pointing in roughly the same direction—then getting out of the way.

I remember getting the community and the institution to share the vision of what Capilano University can be.

I had the privilege of working with truly great people who have inspired me, encouraged me, supported me, corrected me and laughed a lot with me. And that last is very important—it prevents taking yourself too seriously. I found an environment of finding solutions, not creating bureaucracy, and I tried to continue that focus.

I remember the work of all employees—passionate and dedicated faculty, staff and administrators who through good times and tough times have always come through for the students. I remember the series of very fine Boards and exceptional Board Chairs—people who have been overwhelmingly dedicated to providing good governance to the institution. And I remember the remarkable assistance of the special people who worked as both Board and presidential executive support.

I remember the first College baccalaureate degree. It was the first from a college in BC and came about because of the energy and creativity of the faculty and administration

I remember being president of a new university and the support of the community and our elected officials—locally, provincially and federally.

I remember so many people that I daren't try to list them all—so I won't. But there are a few people whom I have to mention. Harold Kirchner and Paul Gallagher, both now deceased, had the faith that a very young physicist could make a contribution. Doug Jardine, one of the most intelligent and principled persons I have ever had the privilege to know, was and is a mentor, a role model, and a friend.

Capilano College, now Capilano University, was and is different. Almost everyone who came to know the institution usually stayed. I did.

MAY 9, 2013: TO FACULTY, STAFF AND STUDENTS

FRANK HARRIS

FOR HALF OF THE 30 years I have taught here I have been involved with governance, first on the Education Council and Budget Committee, and later on the Board of Governors. In that time I have admired many heroes, some of whom you will have seen at the Senate meeting Tuesday afternoon. Speaker after speaker got up and spoke about the damage the proposed cuts will do to students, to diversity, and to Cap's future. Many spoke about the culture of inclusion, of consultation, of cooperation that have made Cap strong in the past, and can make Cap strong again in the future.

Mark Battersby is one of my heroes. He has been working toward a cooperative model of governance at the institution for 40 years. In 1996 he published an article in *The Vancouver Sun* in which he said:

> "Capilano College ... had ... an early recognition by faculty, administration and Board that the College runs better when everyone works together and shares responsibility .... Faculty and administration have jointly explored solutions to funding reductions and increased student demand by reallocating resources and creating a co-management system that requires fewer administrators ... We are not in [a] constant state of labor hostilities punctuated by open conflict ... Both faculty and staff are highly trained professionals and, once given the appropriate respect and responsibility, will deliver the efficient education the public requires." [M. Battersby, 1996 Feb 06, the *Vancouver Sun*]

The following year I was elected to Education Council, and then to the budget committee. The budget committee was composed of two faculty, two students, one staff and one administrator, and was brand new. Every year we faced the issue that the budget projections were initially one or several million dollars short. Costs rise due to inflation, including step increments, computer replacement, parking lot development and repair, cleaning, maintenance, security, increased student demand, other technology, government reporting requirements and so forth. Revenues never rise as quickly. The majority of revenue comes from the provincial government, as do restrictions on the tuition and other fees that Cap can charge.

So how did we deal with the regularly scheduled shortfall? Faculty never wanted administrators to make the reductions. While Cap's finance arm could find creative ways to reduce a lot of costs, the issues of reducing programs and sections, of great importance to students, needed faculty guidance.

The budget committee considered the objectives of the College: diversity, inclusion, and support for the weakest members of society. To measure the success of programs in meeting the objectives we looked at the data available. The province provides a telephone survey of recent graduates every year, with information about employment, satisfaction with programs, instruction, services and so forth. Cap is able to survey current students about use of, and satisfaction with, programs, support services including registration, counselling, the library, learning centres, disability services, use of space, graduation rates, cost per student, etc.

The budget committee selected the relevant data, asked our institutional research arm to collect additional data as we needed it, and put out a grid of data, showing for each program how it came on each of the measures. The jargon for this data is "key performance indicators" or KPI. The data was public, available on the Cap website. Every program, every employee, every student could see how all programs came out on each measurement.

The budget committee then set benchmarks for each measure. If a program failed to reach three or four benchmarks, then the committee looked more closely at the program. Committee members understood that numbers never tell the whole story. Programs often have very good reasons for not meeting several benchmarks.

Usually by about early January the budget committee had sufficient data, and determined which programs required a closer look. The committee sent a letter to each of those programs and asked the program to explain the numbers, to explain why the program had failed on several benchmarks. When possible, the committee gave the program six to eight weeks to respond, to allow time for department meetings, gathering data, and replying with all the defence they could muster.

The program responses were written. The committee wanted data and information that could be written carefully and thoughtfully, supported by data where possible. Only very rarely did the budget committee allow a speaker from a program.

Some programs had very good reasons for not meeting the benchmarks. Others did not.

The budget committee then determined which programs it would recommend for cancellation, to balance the budget. The budget committee made a recommendation to Education Council (currently Senate). At the EC meeting, programs had a chance to defend themselves once again. Very rarely the Senate changed a budget committee recommendation.

Then EC recommended a balanced budget to the Board. The Board received recommendations from Education Council, the president, and each of the 3 unions: faculty, staff and student. And the Board passed the budget.

The process was inclusive, collegial, consultative, open, and provided lots of opportunity for creative minds to find solutions to budget problems. We never had Board meetings full of College members concerned about the decision.

The first time I saw a Board meeting with many University faculty present and angry was in 2011, the first year of President Bulcroft's administration. I am hopeful I will see many concerned employees and students at the Board meeting May 14.

The University has had lots of time to consult since the February 6, 2013 meeting of about 70 people at which provided draft strategic directions. The University had the three months of February, March and April in which to consult: lots of time. We did not need three executive members deciding to cut off the programs they did not like. We did not need the secrecy, lack of consultation, and dictation on what to cut.

We have had "World Cafes" and a "Changemaker Challenge" to get faculty input, but on the most important matter of slashing the University we have had no faculty input. The University community developed a vision, values, mission and goals, but the current cuts do not seem to reference, or reverence, these at all.

We need a major change in process. We need to look at the budget again. I hope we will find a way, a cooperative, consultative, inclusive way forward.

EMAILS ON THE PROGRAM CUTS

PIERRE COUPEY

Wednesday December 19, 2013, to Jane Shackell, CapU Board Chair:

Dear Jane,

Thank you for your courteous response to what was a very short note. The occasion at which we met was quite lovely and I enjoyed meeting you—neither Patti nor I were aware of your pending relationship to Capilano University, and lucky for you: I might have bent your ear. Of course, none of us knew then what was in store for Cap in the final days of the spring term.

Even so, had I known you were to become the Board Chair, I might have said a few words about Cap's traditions of collegiality, the creative genius of faculty, how great an institution it has been, and how supportive the majority of presidents have been of faculty initiatives, innovation and creativity.

Yes, I'm very much aware there were vertical cuts of entire programs, and that there were many cuts to departments and courses in many areas, although very few by contrast in Business or Film. Clearly I'm most concerned with the vertical cuts of programs, especially Studio Art, Textile Arts and the Computer Science department in Arts and Sciences, as they spell the end to three very fine programs. Apparently Studio Art and Interactive Design were well on their way to developing degree-granting programs when they were so suddenly axed without warning, and while faculty were still at work in good faith on developing the degrees.

However, what I, and the majority of the retirees, deplore and condemn is not only the substance of these vertical cuts to programs, but also, and critically, the process by which the cuts were made. They were made unilaterally by the administration without any of the transparent consultation regarding budgets and proposed cutbacks required by historical tradition, the Collective Agreement, and now the University Act.

As I and many others see it, the faculty at large were never given a meaningful opportunity to determine the nature of the required cuts, department by department, division by division, faculty by faculty, as we have in the past.

In the past as faculty we have undergone, on numerous occasions, painful deliberations to determine what to cut where, and we almost always determined to make horizontal cuts throughout the institution rather than to make vertical cuts to entire programs. We always did our best to ensure something of a program remained so growth in that area would be possible if and when budgets improved.

By and large we were almost always successful in doing this, and the proposed cuts were forwarded up the chain: from faculty to department coordinators, from coordinators to division chairs, from chairs to deans, from deans to the executive and the president. The administration trusted, and was guided by, the expertise, the ground knowledge and integrity of the faculty to play a major role in tackling budget crises and cutbacks. And we did the dirty work on the floor.

In spring 2013 this did not happen. In the academic year 2012–2013, this did not happen.

And it should have. There would not be the storm of criticism and disaffection today, among students, faculty, retirees, and the community at large, had such a collegial process been followed. The budget consultation process and determination of cuts to be made should have been a joint faculty / administration collegial process starting in fall 2012. It was not.

You tacitly acknowledge that such was the case when you write, "You are likely aware that in response to some of the criticisms we have faced, *the Board and administration have developed a process to enhance the transparency of decision-making in this difficult area.*" (Emphasis mine.)

I respectfully submit that the words in italics do not inspire the confidence they are meant to. They tacitly yet clearly acknowledge the failure of, and lack of transparency in, the process followed last year by the president and the administration.

The irony is there was / is no *transparency of decision-making in 2012–2013 to enhance,* and yet the process already exists by which transparent decision-making can be made: it is the collegial model. Nor does the top-down emphasis—*the Board and administration have developed*—do anything to assure me that faculty voices are equal partners in this scenario. Yes, the Board and the administration must be leaders, but I would much rather have read the following words: *the Board and administration, in consultation with the faculty, have developed a process to enhance the transparency of decision-making in this difficult area.*

And then, of course, I'd like to know what this process consists of substantially. Is the collegial model being followed now? Are faculty now being fully and respectfully consulted on what cuts must be made in spring 2014? If not there will surely be further distress and criticism.

If, however, by a process you are referring to the deliberations of the Senate budget and advisory committee, with student, staff and faculty representatives, let me say that this is not a process that in any way substitutes for the full consultation with faculty and the CFA that comprises the collegial model.

That the current president apparently refuses to meet directly with the CFA, that the CFA is apparently not allowed to attend Senate budget committee meetings, and the meetings themselves are held in camera, smacks of a high degree of secrecy and a very low degree of transparency. I repeat, the SBAC, no matter how important its role, does not represent transparent and full consultation with the faculty at large.

Because the process leading up to the draconian cuts in spring 2013 was not transparent, was not collegial, was not consultative, this has quite understandably led many to conclude that the president has a hidden agenda. And because the Senate budget and advisory committee meetings are closed, because there isn't full consultation and complete transparency in the budget process now, and because the president refuses to meet and consult with the CFA, and refuses to implement the collegial model, many will conclude that indeed there is a hidden agenda on the part of the president to transform Capilano into a far more narrowly focused institution. This is lamentable, and does not represent serious and good leadership on the part of the president, and must be redressed if any progress is to be made.

Yes, FTE underfunding is a significant factor, but to most of the faculty, who have been repeatedly praised for doing more with less (thanks to the collegial model), it is not the determining factor in the nature of the recent cuts. And because we have always done more with less, Capilano now has a surplus of $12 million to which the provincial government refuses access, either for operating or capital costs, simply to save their political image. This reprehensible political game is played at the expense of Capilano's programs and students, and this must also change if any progress is to be made.

You write the following: *But Cap continues to endure* FTE *funding that is (as you likely know) lower than any other BC university, and lower than some colleges. We also anticipate cuts in our operating grant for the coming year, which will result in more hardship.*

In response to a retired colleague's question regarding FTE underfunding I recently wrote the following: As for the shameful underfunding of Cap by the Ministry:

1. *In part we are our own victims, as out of hubris Cap chose not to take the transitional step of becoming a university-college, as others did, and thereby lost out on an* FTE *increase in funding at that stage.*

2. *When tuition fees were unfrozen, some institutions jacked their fees like crazy. Others, like Cap, decided to phase in tuition hikes. When fees were refrozen, they were frozen at those changed levels, thus again widening the gap between the have institutions and the have-nots, such as Cap. Now a double whammy.*

3. *Alas, when Cap accepted university status, it did so without demanding / securing university level funding.*

4. *Sheer incompetence within the Ministry of Advanced Education itself: over the last 10 years there have been 10 Ministers and 11 Deputy Ministers of Advanced Education. Or so we're told. No one is there long enough, it appears, to do anything real at all, let alone grasp the reporting from 42 institutions province wide, let alone reform the system. If any private enterprise were run with that kind of turnover at the top, it too would likely be a stinking sinking ship . . .*

I may be wrong on all this, but there's obviously a basic issue of fair play and justice here: we should no longer be asked to endure such inequitable FTE funding. Although I believe an FTE is an FTE, no matter what institution in BC, no matter what region of BC, and all should be equally funded, I recognize some programs do cost more to run than others. Nevertheless, within a basic range, all students in BC should be as equally FTE funded as possible, no matter where they go to school. I suspect we might agree on that.

You end your letter with this comment: *I am well aware of your long history of contributions to Capilano; in that spirit, I hope that you will provide your input as part of our process, and that you will advocate for Cap with the public and with government to close our funding gap, rather than requiring program cuts in May 2014.*

I appreciate your invitation to provide input, and hope I have done so in this letter. I, along with the retired faculty, but even more importantly the current faculty, would very much like to be a part of the process, and to again be the advocates for Cap we have always been in the past. None of us enjoy being critics of Cap, but to be true to the spirit of critical thinking we have always taught in our respective disciplines, and to be true to our respect for our democratic traditions at Cap, we cannot be silent when confronted with the failure of leadership we perceive to be occurring at Cap. Nor are we opposed to intelligent change—arrived at by consensus—nor are we nostalgic for what the president referred to as "the golden age of past presidents."

If FTE underfunding is from your perspective the major and critical factor, then it seems to me that we—the Capilano University Board, the Administration, the CFA, the CSU and COPE 378—must eventually come together in common cause to advocate with the government and the Minister of Advanced Education.

The administration and Board were unsuccessful in achieving this last year on their own. Clearly it will take the force of the entire institution and the community to achieve change in this area, and we may have to wait a year or two before the climate for such lobbying becomes positive again, given the failure of last year's efforts.

When the time is right the five representative bodies of Capilano University, plus representatives from the community at large (including retirees), should request an extraordinary meeting with the Minister to negotiate a solution to the chronic FTE underfunding of Cap. And together, the five representative bodies should request a joint meeting with the three North Shore MLAs to enlist their support in hammering out such a solution. Together we may have to mount a public campaign to achieve any change in the funding formula.

In the meantime, however, the present budget processes demand critical attention without the hope of a lifeline, a Hail Mary pass, from the Ministry. What can we do on our own? How can we properly prepare for the mobilization of such a united front?

Good faith must be demonstrated now. To arrive at this positive, unified front, to create a consensus and a common agenda, will require appropriate leadership from the office of the president, and a restoration of mutual trust and confidence.

What the president of Capilano University must demonstrate now, in order to restore trust and confidence, are the following: a willingness to meet with the CFA executive, and to come before a general meeting of the CFA to present in serious and concrete detail (not in terms of abstract "core themes") her "vision" for

CapU; a commitment to ensure the collegial model is scrupulously followed in all budget processes, and that faculty are fully consulted on potential program cuts; and a commitment to ensure immediate CFA attendance at SBAC meetings, and to ensure the meetings are not held in camera, but are transparent and open.

It wouldn't hurt either—in fact it would help immensely—if the president shows she has the grace and intelligence to apologize publicly for the offensive statements regarding faculty she recently made in the *North Shore News*. No president of a university that prides itself on being a *teaching* university can afford to be so careless in her choice of words and so disrespectful of its faculty.

These steps, it seems to me, are the minimum required in order to rebuild a positive direction for Cap. If the current president is unable or unwilling to take these steps, we have no option but to repeat our original call for the Board to remove her from the office, as otherwise it will be impossible to create the unity we need in order to move forward, to make any progress on even the FTE front, let alone build a great Capilano University we can all be proud of and support.

I very much hope you will use your good offices to ensure all possible positive steps are taken to improve governance at Capilano. We hope we will be given the opportunity to put our passion and energy into promoting a unified and well-governed Capilano University in the near future.

This has been a much longer response than I'd planned: please forgive me. I, and several of our retirees, would be more than happy to meet with you to expand upon these points, and we hope you will have time do so in the new year. Please let me know what your schedule permits, and we will make the time to meet with you. What happens at Capilano University is dear to our hearts, aging as they may be now.

Yours sincerely, and in solidarity with the
Capilano University Faculty Retiree Group

Pierre Coupey, BA (McGill), MA (UBC)
Retired Faculty, English department
Founding Editor, *The Capilano Review*
Chair, Capilano Press Society Board
FANS Distinguished Artist 2013

WEDNESDAY FEB 19, 2014, TO BRENT LEIGH, CAPU BOARD MEMBER:

Dear Brent,

Good to see you yesterday and good to have such a candid talk re Cap. Hope the Cap Board meeting went well, and too bad you couldn't be at the Museum Advisory Committee meeting, as the information re the coming show at the West Van Museum guest curated by new Board member Jacqui Wong was fascinating, and underscores how wrong and how out of step Cap's decision to cut Studio and Textile Arts was. How disastrous for NS students, including all those kids who come out of WV.

Her coming show will be called SD45, celebrating the work of graduates in studio arts programs from WV high schools who've gone on to become international art stars: namely Graham Gillmore, Geoffrey Farmer, Ian Wallace, Douglas Coupland, Bobbie Burgers, Ross Penhall, etc., alongside a curated show of work by students, faculty and staff, past & present. Simply amazing. One can imagine such a show focussed on grads of the Studio & Textile Arts programs at Cap . . . .

Now just to review the main points we discussed:

1. Yes, it would be great if the retirees ("the emeritii") could be brought back as supporters of Cap, but for that to happen this president and administration have much to do to restore confidence and trust: real consultation, real transparency, a real commitment to Cap's collegial traditions and comprehensive program offerings. And a real discussion of Cap's future: If Cap continues its slide into being primarily an international business school, which is what we fear is happening, then there might not be much left for us to support.

2. Yes, the retirees represent the first generation of faculty that built Cap, from the ground up, with the support of administration. Good to hear you acknowledge that. Yes, our knowledge of the history of Cap's culture should be valued. If we were First Nations people, no decision at Cap would be made without consulting "the elders" . . . what a concept! And yes we do wish to inspire the next generations at Cap, to help them keep on building a Cap we can all be proud of. However, part of our faculty tradition has been resolute resistance to unilateral and opaque decision-making that excludes faculty, and a refusal to respect bad decisions made behind closed doors. We hope that message is also getting through to the second generation. And stay tuned for the coming faculty anthology.

3. Yes, if we are to make any headway on the structural FTE underfunding of Cap on the part of the Ministry and the government, the administration and Board (which has

> already been punished by the Ministry for strenuous lobbying) must surely realize that politics and business as usual isn't working. Instead, all stakeholders in Cap must be brought together in a united front—Board, admin, faculty, staff, students, community, retirees, MLAs, etc.—to mount a co-ordinated public campaign of education and pressure on the Ministry. Either that or the Board has to resign en masse in protest. Or? Simply accept the status quo?

As for last year's vertical cuts to Studio Art, Textile Art, and Computing Science: to my knowledge all three programs were fully enrolled, and have been for all their years in existence at Cap—in fact the student demand for these programs exceed the places available every year: incoming students in Studio & Textile Art must go through a rigorous interview and selection process. And numerous grads have gone on to complete their 3rd and 4th years at universities across the country. After graduation from Cap's Studio Art program, my own daughter went on to Concordia University where she studied with the great Canadian artist Guido Molinari. None of that would have been possible without Studio Art at Cap, and won't be possible for future generations of North Shore students.

What we must recognize here is that the Studio Art and Textile Art programs at Cap are almost unique in Canada. No other art programs offer quite the same kind of personal and rigorous instruction in hands-on art making: drawing, painting, sculpture and printmaking. Not even Emily Carr teaches original print making in non-digital forms, whereas we do. The Studio Art building is almost a heritage repository of irreplaceable equipment: we have three of the finest print-making presses in western Canada, including one of the largest, if not the largest, and George Rammel has hand-built one of the best bronze sculpture foundries in Western Canada.

Given these technical resources and the faculty expertise to run them, maintain them and teach them, Studio Art has also been able to offer a unique program: the Art Institute in Printmaking and the Art Institute in Sculpture, which allowed graduates and practicing professionals the opportunity to extend their practices through access to this equipment and resources. I myself did the Art Institute in Printmaking for over 5 years and graduated with a certificate. Many of the prints I was able to realize there are now in major public collections, including the Vancouver Art Gallery, the Burnaby Art Gallery and the University of Lethbridge Art Gallery. And soon in the collection of the West Vancouver Museum. So I know first hand, up close and personal, as they say, how valuable these programs are. And I lament profoundly that after this year no one will have access to these irreplaceable educational resources and experiences at Cap.

And neither you nor I really know why they were cut, and according to what criteria. Tragic. And the same applies to Textile Art and Computing Science. Incomprehensible.

And, as I've said often in the past months, these cuts to the Arts at Cap have taken place when at the same time all across the North Shore and the lower mainland the arts are increasingly supported and recognized as essential to the well-being of our communities: we have the new Gordon Smith Gallery for Canadian Art in North Vancouver; the soon to be built new Presentation House Gallery in North Vancouver; the plans for a new Centre for Art, Architecture and Design in West Vancouver, to which you yourself have committed so much energy and time to realize; and a new home for the Vancouver Art Gallery in Vancouver itself. What a crying g**damned shame Capilano University is no longer in a position to be in any way a partner with and a contributor to the flourishing of the [visual] arts in BC, indeed in Canada.

One thing we didn't have time to discuss yesterday was the number of faculty letters sent to the *North Shore News* that didn't get published, all of them deploring the egregious comments the president made regarding "professors blathering." Such comments do not command the respect of faculty, past and present, and demean the very idea of Cap as a teaching university. They also speak volumes to her capacity for intellectual leadership.

I'm enclosing here a link to a recent public statement to the president from Capilano students: they ask some serious questions, the last of which is quite telling: 5. *You announced the closure of the Studio Arts + Textile programs, but many students are still finishing their programs. After they do finish, whatever happens to the Studio Arts building will be seen as a major sign of the direction Cap. U. will be going in. What is your plan for what should happen to that space?* Here's the link: http://goo.gl/p3bcHB

And enclosed below is the very wise and clear proposal from Sandra Ferrens, coordinator Studio Art. It merits a close reading. Somehow something of Studio Art must be saved.

Look forward to hearing from you, perhaps another coffee at Crema?

Cheers,
Pierre

ps Will send you another confidential email, plus forward to you an important email re budget cuts from the CFA.

THURSDAY FEB 20, 2014, TO THE RETIRED FACULTY GROUP:

Dear Colleagues,

Enclosed here is the email I sent yesterday to Brent Leigh, a CapU Board member, subsequent to a Tuesday morning talk re Cap. At his invitation, we met for an informal hour and a half exchange of ideas on the current situation at Cap. He also seems to be concerned with the rationale for cutting Studio and Textile Arts and Computer Science.

He has asked permission to forward my email to the president, and perhaps to the Board, and by the same token I can now forward it to you and keep you informed.

Forgive me for departing from our usual group protocol: normally all our formal communications with the administration are vetted and approved by you in advance. The present circumstances don't allow for this, and I hope I'm representing the views of our group adequately, as well as advancing my own perspectives. I also advanced some further points in two subsequent but confidential emails to him.

At the start of our meeting he informed me that on the CapU Board agenda was the formal Board response to our December 19 letter, and I guess he wanted to suss out our current perceptions of the administration, and as comes clear in my email, he wanted to know what it might take for us as retirees to "rise above" the conflict and re-engage as supporters of Cap. And I think I made it clear to him.

What this might suggest is the following: the Board may well be a bit rattled by our actions, and have come to see that we retirees could be more valuable as allies than antagonists and critics.

And clearly the Board and the admin know they have to clean up their act.

And, as I recently emphasized to Bill and Crof, that makes the coming faculty anthology even more important: it has to be as authoritative as possible, and beautifully made. Yes, we need to have a retiree reunion and book launch, and then do one of these two things: either invite the Board to the launch, or, better? make a special appearance at a Board meeting and present each Board member with a copy of the anthology: and at that time make our statement to the Board re transparency, collegiality, comprehensiveness and academic plan (vision).

This is all happening just as the 2014–2015 budget process is coming to a head. Two things determine our way forward: the nature of Jane Shackell's formal Board response to the December 19 letter (which I hope we receive before the end of term!) and the actualities of the budget cuts that come down in the next weeks. I suggest that both have to be acceptable before we even begin to consider any rapprochements.

I will forward to you by separate email Frank Harris's recent report to the faculty on Tuesday night's Board meeting. It contains key information on the current budget process, and on the Ministry's continuing refusal to address the structural underfunding at Cap.

So that's the update for now. Thoughts, feedback, comments welcome.

Cheers,
Pierre